THE BAFFLED PARENT'S GUIDE TO

COACHING GIRLS'
BASKETBALL

Look for these other Baffled Parent's Guides

Coaching Youth Baseball
by Bill Thurston

Great Baseball Drills
by Jim Garland

Coaching Youth Basketball
by David G. Faucher

Great Basketball Drills
by Jim Garland

Coaching Youth Football
by Paul Pasqualoni with Jim McLaughlin

Youth Football Skills and Drills
by Tom Bass

Teaching Kids Golf
by Detty Moore

Coaching Youth Hockey
by Bruce Driver with Clare Wharton

Coaching Boys' Lacrosse
by Greg Murrell and Jim Garland

Coaching Girls' Lacrosse
by Janine Tucker and Maryalice Yakutchik

Coaching Girls' Soccer
by Drayson Hounsome

Coaching 6-and-Under Soccer
by David Williams and Scott Graham

Coaching Youth Soccer
by Bobby Clark

Great Soccer Drills
by Tom Fleck and Ron Quinn

Coaching Youth Softball
by Jacquie Joseph

Coaching Tee Ball
by Bing Broido

THE BAFFLED PARENT'S

GUIDE TO

Coaching Girls'

BASKETBALL

Sylvia Hatchell

with Jeff Thomas

McGraw-Hill

Camden, Maine • New York • Chicago • San Francisco
Lisbon • London • Madrid • Mexico City • Milan • New Delhi
San Juan • Seoul • Singapore • Sydney • Toronto

*To my loving parents, Veda Shepard Rhyne (died 12/22/04)
and Carroll Costner Rhyne, from whom I learned countless valuable
lessons, and built my life and and success on their faith, hope, and love.*

*And to my husband, Carl (Sammy) Hatchell,
and my son, Van Davis Hatchell, the loves of my life.*
—Sylvia Hatchell

To Jana, the best teammate I know.
—Jeff Thomas

The **McGraw·Hill** Companies

10 9 8 7 6 5 4 3 2 1 DOC DOC 9 8 7 6 5

© 2006 by Sylvia Hatchell

Library of Congress Cataloging-in-Publication Data
Hatchell, Sylvia.
  The baffled parent's guide to coaching girls' basketball / Sylvia Hatchell with Jeff Thomas.
      p.   cm.
  Includes index.
  ISBN 0-07-145923-5 (pbk. : alk. paper)
  1. Basketball for girls—Coaching. I. Thomas, Jeff, 1949– II. Title.
  GV885.3.H38 2005
  796.323'8—dc22   2005026456

Questions regarding the content of this book should be addressed to
McGraw-Hill/Ragged Mountain Press
P.O. Box 220
Camden, ME 04843
www.raggedmountainpress.com

Questions regarding the ordering of this book should be addressed to
The McGraw-Hill Companies
Customer Service Department
P.O. Box 547
Blacklick, OH 43004
Retail customers: 1-800-262-4729
Bookstores: 1-800-722-4726

Photographs by Bruce Curtis

Contents

Part One Coaching 101: The Coach's Start-Up Kit

Introduction: Now That I'm a Coach, What's Next?

Out of the blue, at the parents' meeting, someone says, "Hey, we need a coach for the youth league girls' team. Do you have any experience?" Before you can say, "None at all," someone hands you a whistle and a clipboard.

So here you are, the rookie coach of a girls' basketball team, wondering "What's next?"

In this book, I explain how to teach footwork, dribbling, passing, shooting, and all the things you'll need to know about coaching your team. It all starts with the fundamentals. For any team to succeed, whether it's a youth team or a professional team, *the coach must focus on fundamentals.* When we start practices every year at North Carolina, though we have talented players who have played basketball for years, we spend the first several days on nothing but fundamentals.

This book is based on the knowledge and insight I've gained over many years of coaching. My focus is on how to coach girls 6 to 12 years old—that is, girls who play youth and middle school basketball. If you coach at the younger end of those ages, some of the skills and drills I've included will be too advanced for your players. The drills in Part Two of this book are labeled beginner, intermediate, and advanced.

Are you ready? You're about to take your first steps as a coach. I hope you find coaching basketball as fulfilling, enjoyable, and exciting as I do!

The Coach's Role

When you walk into the gym for the first practice and see twelve eager faces, you become aware of how much the girls are counting on you. Their expectations are huge. They may be nervous and scared, but you're their leader, the all-knowing coach who will ease their fears and make everything good. Think not? Look at those faces. Whether you realize it or not, you're on a pedestal. You're their role model. What you do and teach is the gospel. If you say the sky is made of caramel, then it must be true.

The influence you have is a great opportunity and a great responsibility. It's incumbent that you use this influence wisely. Your players will note everything you do and say. How you handle pressure, how you handle referees, how you treat each player, how you treat the team as a whole—the girls will see you in roles they don't see their parents in. They'll model their behavior after yours. More than your words, more than the number of wins and losses, your actions will determine how successful the season is.

What's involved in being a coach? What do you do? How much do you have to learn?

The answer to all these questions is: "More than you ever imagined." You'll soon become aware of how multifaceted coaching is. To lead a successful team, you must master many aptitudes and be many things.

Coach Hatchell in action.

Possessor of All Knowledge

You don't have to be John Wooden or Dean Smith, but you must have a working knowledge of the game. "Whoa," you say in a panic, "I hardly know anything about basketball!" That's fine. You can learn. (I assume that's why you're reading this book.) Talk to other coaches. Attend clinics. Search the Internet. Read more books and study tapes. There's a ton of information out there, and most of it's easy to find.

Still feeling a lack of confidence? Find someone who knows something about the game and make him or her your assistant. Better yet, find two assistants. Having the help of one or two people who know what they're doing will quickly make you a knowledgeable head coach. At the least, your girls will *think* you know everything. They might be in the dark as to the actual level of your expertise, but that's fine. You'll be surprised at how fast you learn as the season progresses.

Teacher

It's one thing to know how to shoot a layup. It's another thing to teach it. As mentioned above, the first requirement of good teaching is that you know your subject. The second requirement is that you know how to communicate what you know.

Some coaches are natural communicators and some aren't. If you're the latter, the good news is that this is a skill anyone can learn. Brevity is important. When addressing kids, keep it short and sweet. The attention span of girls is limited. Droning on for more than a minute or two wastes time you could use to develop skills. Feed your girls information in short, easy bites. Don't overwhelm them with too much new information.

Becoming a good teacher takes time. The more you coach, the better you'll be.

Director of Player Personnel

Handling players well is crucial to establishing team unity.

Rule number one: *Be consistent.* You can't treat your players one way one day and another way the next day. You can't enforce discipline one time but not the next. Mixed signals cause confusion. Kids respond to structure and consistency.

Rule number two: *Don't play favorites.* Though it's natural for you to enjoy certain personalities more than others, you can't treat one player more favorably than another. Coaches who play favorites cause negative feelings and a lack of trust. No player should think she's a second-class citizen, that certain players can bend the rules and she can't; nor should a player think that she has special privileges or authority over other players.

Motivator

Many books are dedicated to the subject of how to encourage and inspire a group of people to put aside their personal interests for a common goal. There are no sure-fire methods for motivating players that ensure success. You'll find this aspect of coaching frustrating at times. If you discover that you're good at it, your job will be much easier, and your team will be well on its way to a successful season.

Puzzle Master

Putting together a successful team is like putting together a complicated puzzle. It might seem that there are only a limited number of pieces (the number of players on your team), but the puzzle becomes difficult when, as the season progresses, the pieces change shape. Young players develop physically and emotionally at different rates. Your team might experience unexpected roster changes. You may have players who decide to leave the team or who get sick or injured. What looks like a finished puzzle in December can look like a jumble of scattered pieces in January. Good coaches adapt to the changing puzzle.

Grand Planner

Basketball is a difficult game to learn. Dribbling under pressure, one of the many skills a player must learn, takes constant repetition over time. Most youth and middle school teams practice two or three times a week, which creates interesting decisions for the coach. How much time should I spend in practice on fundamentals versus team skills? How much time should I spend on shooting versus rebounding? How much time should I devote to offense versus defense?

The formula that works for one team might not work for another. Plan your practices based on the strengths and weaknesses of your players, the competition you'll face, and the allotted preparation time. Some players learn faster than others, so you'll have to decide whether to continue teaching new things or to slow the process so everyone on the team can absorb them. It's a tricky balancing act. You didn't realize there's so much to coaching girls' basketball, did you?

X's and O's Guru

If you aren't familiar with the X's and O's of basketball, you'll need to bone up fast. This is part of knowing your subject, but it goes beyond fundamentals into the area of strategies and tactics. You have critical decisions to make early in the season. Should we play man-to-man defense or zone defense? What offenses should we run? What inbound plays? How should we set up to break the presses we'll face?

There are as many X's and O's as there are coaches, and you don't have time to waste. Start boning up now. The first game is only a few weeks away.

Bench Coach

By the time the first game arrives, you've either done a good job of getting your team ready to play or you haven't. Over the next hour, you'll find out if your players are ready to face defensive pressure, are in good basketball condition, and will remember to run those special plays. You won't know how prepared they are until the game is underway, but one thing is certain—the decisions you make during the game will have a big impact on the outcome.

Who should start? Who should be the first player off the bench? When should you switch from zone to man-to-man defense? When should you call a time-out, and what should you say? The decisions a coach makes during a game often decide whether the team wins or loses.

Parent Handler

Someone once said, "If you want to please everyone, don't go into coaching." Amen.

Most parents are supportive, enthusiastic, reasonable people. They appreciate the unpaid time you give to coaching their daughter. They understand that basketball isn't the most important thing in the world, that it's just a kids' game.

However, if you're like most coaches, you'll encounter some parents whose perspective is different. Sooner or later, you'll have to listen to an unhappy parent. The usual issue is playing time. If your team belongs to a league that mandates equal playing time, you're less likely to run into that

Ask the Coach

Question: My daughter is on my team, and she's the best player. How should I handle this?

Answer: A parent who coaches his or her daughter is in a difficult situation that often leads to problems. My first caution concerns your statement that your daughter is the "best player." Are you sure? Would people who know basketball agree with you? If you give your daughter more playing time than you give other players, and their parents don't perceive her the way you do, you'll cause resentment. Many parents are incapable of viewing their daughters through an objective lens. No matter what you do, some parents will be quick to conclude that you favor your daughter over theirs. *The best thing for you and your daughter is for you not to be her coach.* If you're determined to do so anyway, thinking you'll be smart enough to avoid the pitfalls, go out of your way not to favor her. Of course, don't overcompensate and treat her less favorably than you treat the other girls. That would be unfair to her.

Having your daughter on your team is tricky. Decisions you make regarding her will be under constant scrutiny, sometimes by unreasonable people. My advice is to avoid this situation.

problem. Some coaches stipulate that they'll talk to parents about everything except playing time. Other coaches will discuss the issue with parents. Regardless of how you decide to handle it, develop a thick skin and an ability to defuse the situation. Listen like a psychiatrist and talk like a diplomat. No matter how unreasonable the parent is, be calm and professional. Above all, don't take it personally.

Coaching girls' basketball can be one of the most rewarding, exciting, and fun things you'll ever do, but make no mistake—it's a challenge. The extent of your success will depend on how well you learn the skills and roles listed above.

Good luck!

Developing a Philosophy and a Style

Decide early on what kind of coach you're going to be. Do you prefer to coach an aggressive team that attacks on offense and defense, that gambles and takes chances, or do you prefer to control the action, to slow the pace, and to call specific plays every possession? In other words, will you be a fast-break coach or a half-court-oriented coach? Will your team play a pressure man-to-man defense or a more passive zone defense where you wait for the other team to make mistakes? What style best suits your personality and your players' skills?

I like a running style. It's fun for the players to play and for the fans to watch. Other coaches prefer a slower-paced game. They like to control the action and aren't comfortable with the helter-skelter aspect of fast-break basketball. Every coach is different. Only you can decide what style of play you're most comfortable with.

Consider the skill level and experience of your players. You may want to play a running style, but if your team is slower than your opponent's, this style probably won't work. This past season, I decided to trim our playbook because we had too many offensive strategies. I thought my team needed to spend more time on fewer things. Though you may stay with the same basic philosophy each season, you still have to adapt to the players you have. Good coaches adjust their playing style as needed.

What Are Your Goals?

If you ask most new coaches what their goal is, you'll likely hear, "To win as many games as possible."

Take the time to determine a clear set of coaching goals. Goals are the basis for the organizing and planning you'll do. It's fine to want your team to win all its games—what coach doesn't want that?—but there are many components to achieving success. Most have nothing to do with wins and losses.

If you make the game fun, you'll have a happy team.

One of the main goals I have every season is to help our team reach its potential. Every year is different, of course. Some years, I think we have the potential to be a Final Four team. Other years, if we make the NCAA Tournament, that would be a great accomplishment. I've had teams that have won twenty-five games, but I've thought that we should have done better. Then, I've had teams that won sixteen games, and I've thought we went far along the path to our potential.

You have to decide what goals make sense to you. Here are the goals I'd have if I were in your shoes:

Make sure each player has a positive season. This should be your number one goal. If, at the end of the season, every player, from your best player to the player at the end of the bench, had a season that made her feel good, you did an excellent job. Accomplishing this isn't easy, as you'll learn, but you should keep it at the forefront of your mind. The season isn't about you or a few select players. It's about every girl on the team.

Make basketball fun. You're probably dealing with players with little or no experience. If you insist on a military-like atmosphere, you'll be in a losing battle. Find a balance in practice between working hard and having fun. Every now and then, have the kids play games like Knockout (Drill 39) and Dribble Tag (Drill 15). Divide them into teams and have them run relay dribble races and shooting competitions. If your players think basketball is fun, they'll work harder than if they think it's a chore. If they have a positive, fun experience on your team, they'll be eager to play again next year.

Emphasize fundamentals. It's more important that you teach your players how to play the game, as opposed to a countless number of plays. Spend at least half of each practice on the basics. Your girls are at the perfect age to learn good habits. It's your job to make sure that by the time they reach high school, they have good shooting form and know how to pivot, how to pass to the post, how to play defense, and so on. As part of this goal, before the season begins, develop a list of skills you want your players to learn (see the sample master practice plan in the Appendix).

Instill good work habits. Very few girls aged 6 to 12 know how to work hard. Insist on a good work ethic from the first practice on. Make sure your players run to you when you raise your hand or call to them. If you allow them to dawdle, to saunter on over, it will take longer to move from one drill to the next. If you don't establish the right tone at the beginning, it will be hard to change your players' behavior later.

Coach improvement. It's popular to think that if a team wins a lot, it's because of great coaching, and if a team loses a lot, it's because of bad coaching. The real mark of good coaching isn't how many games are won

Ask the Coach

Question: My team is in a slump. We've lost three games in a row, and no matter what I do, I can't seem to get them out of it. They don't look like they're having fun anymore. What can I do?

Answer: Forget about winning for now. Your players take their cues from you. If you're overly disappointed about losing, they'll hear it in your tone and see it in your body language. They'll think you're disappointed in them as people. Review your coaching goals. Concentrate on improvement. Don't be too hard in practice. Have them play some team games next practice. Put the fun back into it. The more they see you smiling, enjoying them, the better they'll feel about themselves.

or lost, but how much the players and team improve over the season. Being a coach is like being dealt a hand of cards in a poker game. Sometimes you're holding kings and aces, and sometimes you're holding low cards. You have no control over the talent on your team. The true measure of coaching is what the coach does with the hand he or she is dealt. If your players improve and the team improves, you've done a fine job.

Teach sportsmanship. Talk to your players about good sportsmanship. Teach them how to win and lose with dignity and grace. Teach them to treat their teammates, their opponents, the referees, and their coaches with respect. Teach them how to behave in a first-class manner. By doing do, you'll be teaching them far more than basketball.

Teach life lessons. Sports are a wonderful opportunity to learn life skills. You can use your influence to teach your players things much more important than how to shoot. Every team goes over bumpy roads. By your actions and words, show your players how to overcome adversity, how to stick together, how to never give up, and how to work hard for a common purpose. Don't get so wrapped up in the X's and O's that you forget to pass on important values. Basketball lessons last for a season. Life lessons last forever.

Win as many games as possible. Here it is, at the end of the list. Of course it's important, but you'll find that if you achieve the other goals on this list, the wins and losses will take care of themselves.

Coaching Girls Versus Coaching Boys

There are significant differences in coaching girls versus coaching boys.

You might be surprised to learn that these differences aren't based on

Ask the Coach

Question: I'm a guy coach who has coached only boys. Would I be better suited to coaching a boys' team instead of a girls' team?

Answer: It depends. If you approach coaching girls the same way you approach coaching boys, you might have a hard time relating to girls. However, if you adapt your approach for the differences, there's no reason why you can't be a good girls' coach.

Girls can go after rebounds as tenaciously as boys can.

the obvious physical contrasts. What makes coaching girls different than coaching boys is that girls and boys have different emotional and psychological characteristics. Your chances of being a successful girls' coach will improve when you learn how to adapt your approach so you can best relate to, motivate, and teach your girls.

Most coaches who've coached boys and girls agree on the following generalizations (as with all generalizations, there are plenty of exceptions):

Boys don't take constructive criticism personally. Girls do. Girls are sensitive. For many of your girls, this will be the first time that someone besides their parents and their teachers corrects them and tells them what to do. If you're too harsh, or if you correct a player too much (in her mind, not yours), you may find you have an unhappy player.

Boys are naturally aggressive. Girls aren't. Many girls won't get that killer instinct you're looking for during the whole season. Some won't ever get it. You'll find that girls who play in the driveway with their brothers will be used to the physical contact that occurs in basketball (these girls are often your best players). For the beginners, it will take a while before they don't shy away from the roughness of the game. Again, patience is the password to success.

Boys think of themselves first. Girls think of themselves last. A boys' coach has to tell the players to pass more and not hog the ball. A girls' coach has to tell the players to pass less, that they're missing opportunities for good shots. This is a good thing. Many girls' teams become excellent passing teams.

Boys think playing in games is the best part of the season. Girls think being part of a team is the best part. Girls like the camaraderie and the closeness of being on a team. They like working together and helping each other succeed. This provides you with a great opportunity to have a team with good *chemistry.* That's not to say all the players on your team will be close, but the odds are your team will have unity and cohesion.

Boys don't mind if a coach yells at them. Girls do. The marine sergeant approach doesn't usually work in girls' basketball. This isn't to say you can't raise your voice. There are times you'll need to so your players can hear you. Shouting instructions from the sidelines, as long as you're not berating a player, won't hurt anyone's feelings. However, negative shouting will embarrass a player, may alienate her, and may cause other players to perceive you negatively.

How to Use This Book

This is a reference book, a how-to book packed with information, best read in small chunks. Use it to prepare for the season, to coach your team during the season, and to evaluate how you did after the season ends.

The book has more information than you'll need. If you coach very young players, pick and choose what to teach. Limit the information you give your players. They can only absorb so much.

Part One covers all the basics to get you started, including the rules of the game, practice planning, teaching fundamental skills, teaching offensive and defensive strategies, and game preparation and strategies.

Part Two contains drills you can use to teach the various skills. Each drill is marked with a degree of difficulty designation so you can choose the ones that best fit your team:

☞ *beginner*

☞ *intermediate*

☞ *advanced*

To make it easy to understand the concepts, plays, offenses, defenses, and drills presented in the book, I've included many diagrams. The diagrams use the following symbols:

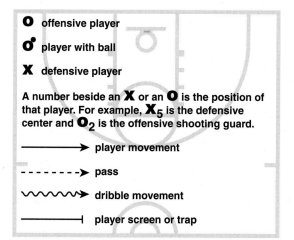

O offensive player

O' player with ball

X defensive player

A number beside an **X** or an **O** is the position of that player. For example, **X$_5$** is the defensive center and **O$_2$** is the offensive shooting guard.

⟶ player movement

- - - - -⟶ pass

〰〰〰⟶ dribble movement

⊢ player screen or trap

Diagram key.

Throughout the book, I introduce many basketball terms and phrases. Some are self-explanatory, but others require explanation. Part of becoming a good coach is talking like a good coach. If you come across a term or phrase that you don't know and that isn't explained in the text, check the glossary in the Appendix.

I've included a number of question-and-answer Ask the Coach sidebars to cover related topics.

The Appendix also includes a sample practice plan, a sample player-parent handout, and a guide to referee signals, among other things. The index will help you locate advice on specific topics.

Are you ready to learn how to coach girls' basketball? If so, take a deep breath and forge ahead!

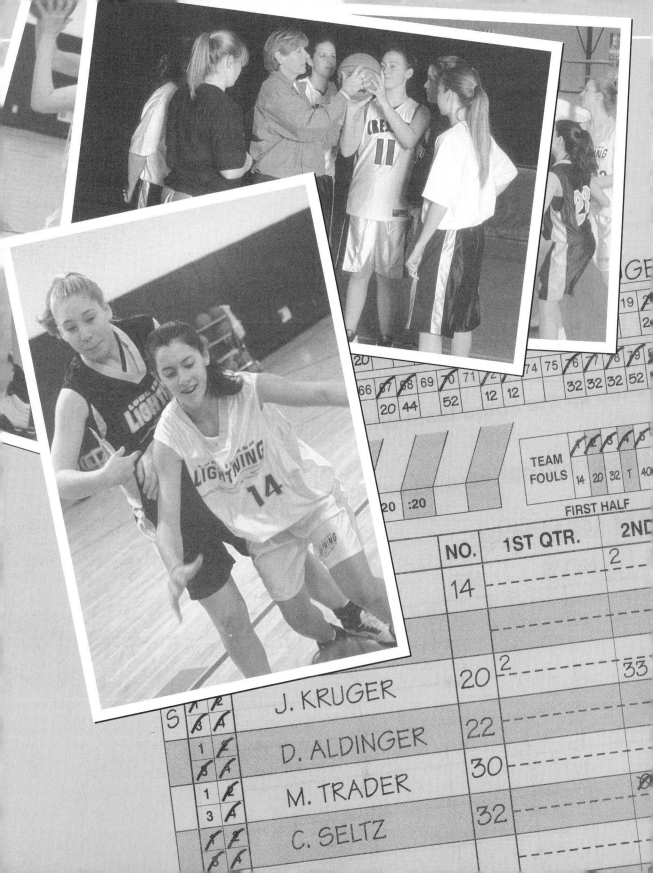

		NO.	1ST QTR.	2ND
				2
		14		
S	⟋⟍	20	2	33
J. KRUGER				
D. ALDINGER		22		
M. TRADER		30		
C. SELTZ		32		

PART ONE

Coaching 101:
The Coach's Start-Up Kit

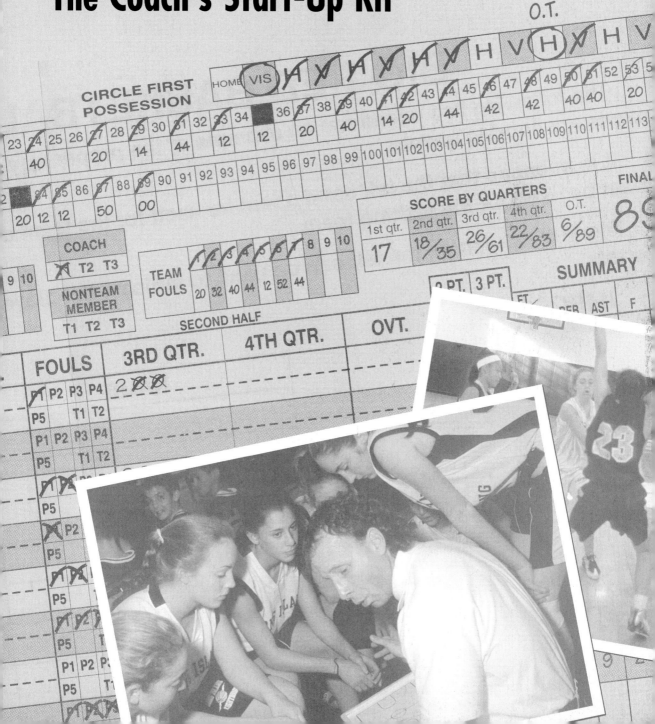

Preparing for the Season

Before you can coach basketball, you need to have a working knowledge of the rules of the game, starting with where it's played.

About the Game

The Court

Basketball is played on a surface called a *court*. The court can be indoors or outdoors, though youth and middle school courts are usually indoors. The surface can be made of wood, concrete, or asphalt. Some courts are carpeted, and some have hard rubber surfaces. Many outdoor courts around the world are simply patches of hard dirt with a basket. The best (and most expensive) courts are made of maple wood.

College courts are 94 feet long and 50 feet wide. The dimensions of youth league and middle school courts vary.

Basic Rules

Basketball is a complicated game with many rules. It will take game experience before you learn everything you need to know. Here are the basics:

Object of the game. As with most other team sports, the team with the most points at the end of the game wins.

The ball. You'll use the women's size ball, which is 28.5 inches in circumference. All the major manufacturers, such as Wilson and Spalding, sell this size in both indoor and outdoor versions. You can buy balls at most sporting goods outlets.

Number of players and substitutions. There are five players on the court for each team at the same time. You can substitute fresh players at any time, from one player up to five. There are no limitations on how many times you can substitute and how many times a player can come in and out of the game. Substitutions can be made only on a *dead ball*, when the referee blows the whistle and play stops. You can substitute after the first of two free

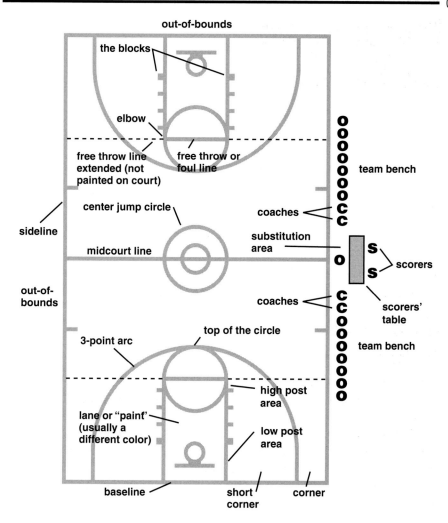

The basketball court.

throws and after the last free throw, but you can't substitute before the first free throw. The only player for whom you can't substitute is the player shooting at the free throw line.

Time. The length of the game varies, depending on the age level. High school games last 32 minutes, divided into 8-minute quarters. Middle school and youth league games are usually shorter and also divided into quarters. Some leagues use a *running clock*, meaning the clock doesn't stop when the referee stops play. The time between quarters is usually 1 minute, and the time between halves is usually 5 minutes.

The baskets. Each basket consists of a rim with a net attached to a *backboard*, which is attached to a structural support, such as a pole. Some baskets are fixed in place, and some can be raised to the ceiling to get them out of the way. The standard height for the rim is 10 feet off the floor. Each team has its *own basket*, a basket they defend. Each team sits on one side of the *scorers' table*. At the start of a game, each team's basket is the one near the team bench, and the team tries to score at the far basket. At halftime, the teams *switch baskets*; each team now defends the far basket and tries to score at the near basket.

Scoring. When a player scores from anywhere inside the 3-point arc, it counts as 2 points. Any shot made from outside the 3-point arc counts as 3 points. For a shot to be considered a 3-point shot, the shooter's feet must not touch the 3-point arc. If a shooter's toe is on the line, the shot is a 2-point shot. Two-point shots and 3-point shots are *field goals. Free throws*, awarded to a player who has been fouled, are shot from the *free throw line*, or *foul line*. Successful free throws are worth 1 point. If a team mistakenly scores in the wrong basket (yes, this sometimes happens with young players), the basket counts for the other team.

Moving the ball. A team that has possession of the ball tries to move the ball close to the other team's basket for a good scoring opportunity. Players advance the ball by *dribbling* (bouncing the ball on the floor with one hand) and *passing* (throwing) it to a teammate, subject to certain rules. When players throw the ball at the basket to try to score, they are *shooting*. As noted above, different kinds of successful shots *(made shots)* result in scoring 1 to 3 points.

Defending the basket. When a team doesn't have possession of the ball, it defends its own basket. Players are allowed to gain possession of the ball from the other team by stealing passes, stealing dribbles, and getting defensive rebounds. A good defensive team makes it hard for the offensive team to dribble, pass, or shoot.

Rules about Fouls

The rules about fouls are designed to keep the game from getting too rough and to penalize players who violate the rules. One of the referee's main duties is to enforce the rules about fouls. Each time a foul is committed, the referee stops play. The referee gives the appropriate hand signal to indicate what the foul was and calls out the number of the player who committed the foul and the type of foul ("Number 32 . . . push"). (See the referee hand signals in the Appendix.)

Personal fouls happen when a player makes physical contact with an opponent in a manner not allowed by the rules. A defender can foul a player with the ball or without the ball. When she fouls a player who is shooting, it's a *shooting foul*. If the shot scores, the referee signals *and one*, which means the shooter also gets awarded one free throw. If the shot misses, the shooter is awarded two free throws in the case of a 2-point shot and three free throws in the case of a 3-point shot.

When a defender fouls a player who is not in the process of shooting, it's a *nonshooting foul*. The penalty for a nonshooting foul is a *change of possession*. The team that was fouled *inbounds* the ball, that is, an *inbounder* passes the ball to a teammate from a spot outside the court boundaries. The spot is along the nearest line to where the foul occurred.

The following are the most common nonshooting fouls.

Reaching across a player's body with your arm

Holding a player (any part of her, including her jersey)

Pushing a player (with any part of your body)

Tripping a player

Blocking a player who is driving to the basket by getting in her way and knocking her off her path

A player on offense can also commit an *offensive foul*. She can commit a *charge* when she dribbles into a defender who has established position. This is one of the more difficult calls a referee has to make. Was it a charge or a block? Whichever way the referee calls it, one of the coaches will disagree.

There are three other kinds of personal fouls:

An *intentional foul* happens when a player makes illegal contact and isn't trying to go for the ball. Intentional fouls result in two free throws being awarded.

A reaching foul.

A *flagrant foul* is called for excessive roughness, such as punching. It seldom happens, but when it does, the referee has the right to remove the offending player from the game.

A *technical foul* can be assessed to a player or a coach (this means you!), at the referee's discretion, for various unsportsmanlike actions, including profanity, insulting the referee, and throwing the ball at a player. A technical foul is also assessed when the defender reaches across the imaginary plane of the baseline while guarding an inbounder. The penalty for a technical foul is for a player on the other team (any player the coach chooses) to shoot free throws without anyone standing along the lane. Then the shooter's team inbounds the ball from their end of the court. Obviously, technical fouls can be very costly to a team.

Each player is allowed five personal fouls per game. When a player commits her fifth foul, she *fouls out*. She must leave the game immediately, and the coach must put in a substitute player for her. Players who foul out can't come back into the game.

Know at all times how many fouls each of your players has. If a player accumulates fouls quickly, or is in danger of fouling out, take her out so she'll be available to play later in the game. Also, keep track of the individual fouls for the other team. You might want one of your players to dribble at a defender who's in foul trouble in the hopes of the defender fouling out of the game.

Team fouls are the total number of the personal fouls each team accumulates during a half. At the end of the first half, the team foul total for each team resets to zero. Once a team commits its seventh team foul in a half, the other team is *in the bonus*. This means the other team is awarded a *one-and-one* on any nonshooting foul that occurs during the rest of the half. The fouled player shoots one free throw. If she makes it, she shoots another free throw. Once a team commits its tenth team foul, the other team is awarded a *two-shot free throw* for every nonshooting foul. Every player fouled now shoots two free throws, even if she misses the first one.

Fouls are a huge factor in games. A team that fouls a lot puts itself at a big disadvantage. It risks losing players and gives the other team free chances for extra points. Conversely, a team that knows how to play good defense without fouling is tough to score on. A team with good free throw shooters has an advantage over a team that shoots poorly from the line. Often close games are decided by who wins the "Battle of the Free Throw Line."

Other Rules

Here are the other basic rules of the game. If a player on your team violates any of these rules, your team gives up possession of the ball.

- **10-second backcourt call.** Once a player inbounds the ball in the backcourt, her team must advance it past the midcourt line within 10 seconds.
- **Closely guarded call.** A player with the ball who is guarded by a defender within 6 feet of her must advance the ball within 5 seconds. This prevents one player from dribbling in one spot as a stalling tactic.
- **5-second call.** A player who picks up her dribble must pass or shoot within 5 seconds.
- **5-second call on the inbounder.** An inbounder must pass the ball to a teammate within 5 seconds.
- **3-second lane call.** An offensive player can't stay in the lane for more than 3 seconds. She has to keep moving in and out of the area. If the ball is shot and hits the rim, the count starts over.
- **Moving pick.** A screener can't move after setting a screen.
- **Over-and-back call.** After bringing the ball over the midcourt line into the frontcourt, a team can't take the ball back over the line into the backcourt.
- **Traveling.** A dribbler can't take more than one step without dribbling.
- **Double dribble.** A player can't dribble with both hands more than once.
- **Carrying.** A player dribbling the ball can't bring her hand underneath it and briefly "palm" or "carry" the ball.

A *held ball* occurs when a defender grabs the ball while it's in the hands of the offensive player, and neither player can yank it away. While the other violations result in an automatic change of possession, a held ball uses an *alternating possession* system. Regardless of which team is on offense and which team is on defense, possession of the ball alternates between the two teams following a held ball.

Most scorers' tables have a box that displays a red LED arrow, or a mechanical pointer used as an arrow. The arrow points to one basket or the other. The clock keeper is in charge of the arrow. At the beginning of the game, the arrow is neutral. If team A gets possession of the ball off the center jump, the rules consider that team A has used its possession, and the clock keeper points the arrow in the direction of team A's basket. That means that on the next held ball, team B gets the ball. Team B inbounds the ball along the nearest point on the sideline or baseline where the held ball occurred. As soon as team B inbounds, the clock keeper switches the arrow so that team A will get the next held ball.

Palming, or carrying, the ball. A player can't do this while dribbling.

The Positions

Basketball players fall into in one of two general categories: *guards* (or *perimeter players*), who play away from the basket, and *forwards* (or *posts*), who play near the basket.

The terms that coaches use to refer to the positions have changed over the years. The old terminology has evolved into numbers. Instead of talking about the *shooting guard*, coaches now talk about the *two guard* or the *2*. It doesn't matter which terminology you use as long as you're consistent.

Point Guard or 1 The point guard is the most important position on the team. If you have a good point guard, your team will have a good chance of succeeding. The point guard is your *floor leader*. She helps direct the offense. Put your best ball handler at the point. Ideally, she should be able to dribble with either hand, with her head up, and should be a good passer. She should have good *court savvy*—she should know when to pass, when to *drive* (attack the basket with the dribble), when to shoot, when to slow things down, and when to speed things up. She's often the quickest player on the team.

Shooting Guard or 2 The shooting guard should be your best outside shooter. She should be able to shoot not just when catching the ball but also off the dribble. If she can also fake the shot and drive, so much the better.

Small Forward or 3 The small forward may not be as good a ball handler as the guards, but she should be able to protect the ball from quicker defenders. Any outside shooting ability is a plus, but she should be able to drive to the basket for close-in shots and offensive rebounds. If she's tall, she should look to pass over the defense when possible.

Power Forward or 4 The power forward should be your best inside scorer.

Question: Help! I don't have any tall girls on my team. What should I do?

Answer: If you coach young girls, you're likely to have a team of guards. You can still have a competitive team. Find your toughest, most aggressive rebounders and put them inside. Find your quickest players and put them outside. Find your best ball handler and put her at point. Your team will be fine. Most of the teams you'll play will also have short players. Even if they have tall players, most tall players at that age are still slow and awkward.

Question: I have a few players who can dribble well enough, but none of them want to play point guard. They say it's too much pressure. How do I make a point guard out of reluctant players?

Answer: Not without patience and salesmanship. Playing point guard requires a level of confidence few young players have. Developing confidence takes time. Focus on your two best dribblers, and talk to them together. Tell them the team needs two people to start the offense, and ask them to share the duties. They will alternate being on the court. By cutting the responsibility in half, their anxiety and reluctance should decrease. If you're lucky, one of them may decide playing point guard is a good thing.

She should be strong and an aggressive rebounder. She should be a good free throw shooter because she'll go to the free throw line often.

Center or 5 The center is usually the tallest player on the team. She should be the best rebounder. If you play a zone defense, she should guard the middle of the lane. She must know how to fight for position. She should be comfortable with rough, physical play.

Setting Up the Season

Team Equipment

Before your first practice, you'll need to acquire the following items:

- **Balls.** Get enough balls so each player can use one at the same time. There's no reason to buy the most expensive balls. Medium-priced balls bounce just as high.
- **Ball bag.** There are two types: see-through mesh bags with a drawstring, and canvas bags with carrying handles. The mesh bags are much cheaper.
- **Ball pump.** If you can afford an electric pump, get one; they're easier to use than hand pumps. Either way, buy lots of extra needles, because they break frequently.
- **Pinnies.** Buy three colors of these mesh-style jerseys, six of each, for drills such as Three-on-Three-on-Three (Drill 65). Make sure the pinnies are washed often (wash them yourself or assign this duty to an assistant).
- **Medicine kit.** If your school or league doesn't provide a medicine kit, create one. Buy a hard plastic box with a carrying handle (a fishing tackle

box or toolbox), along with bandages of different sizes, gauze, splints, antibacterial first-aid cream, scissors, nonaspirin pain reliever, and plastic bags for ice. If you don't have an ice machine where you practice, buy some ice packs (the kind you activate by snapping the pack). Most basketball injuries require ice right away.

- **Scorebook.** These are available at any good sporting goods store.
- **Whistle on a lanyard.** Some coaches like to use whistles, and some don't. We use them in our scrimmages to make things more gamelike. All players understand that when they hear a whistle, they should stop what they're doing. If you're going to use a whistle, use it sparingly.
- **Clipboard.** These come as whiteboard types that have a diagram of the court printed on them or as the old-style pressed wood types. Buy the whiteboard type. You'll need it to illustrate plays to the team during the games. Buy extra dry-erase markers.
- **Rule book.** I've covered most of the rules of the game above, but there are other rules you need to know. The rule book comes in handy as a reference guide when you're unsure of a particular call.
- **Uniforms.** Players love to wear uniforms, and the snazzier, the better. Ideally, you'll have two sets: home (white) and away (colored). Most youth and middle school teams have only one set. If that's your situation, the set should be colored. Be sure to have some Large sizes and one or two Extra-Large sizes. It's embarrassing for a girl who's overweight or large for her age to have to squeeze into pair of shorts two sizes too small.

Player Equipment

Players should wear a clean T-shirt, clean shorts, and basketball shoes to practice. The latter is particularly important; tennis shoes, running shoes, and regular sneakers don't provide the ankle support that basketball shoes do.

Players should also bring their own water bottle, which helps protect

Ask the Coach

Question: I keep trying to pump up our balls, but the needles keep snapping off. Is there a trick to it?
Answer: Yes. Before you put the needle into the hole, moisten the tip with a bit of saliva. Then the needle will slide in easily. Also, as you pump, hold the needle in place so it doesn't wobble back and forth.

Question: I noticed that the numbers on our uniforms don't go over 5. What's wrong with having higher numbers like football teams do?
Answer: When the referees call fouls, they use their hands to signal the player's number. If they call number 23 for a reaching foul, they'll hold up two fingers on one hand and three fingers on the other. That's why 55 is the highest number you'll ever see on a basketball uniform.

them from any germs they might pick up from drinking at the gym water fountain.

Finally, your players should bring any medical equipment they need, such as an inhaler or ankle braces.

You should list these responsibilities in your player-parent handout (see the sample in the Appendix).

What to Do in Tryouts: The Big Picture

Some youth and middle school teams don't have tryouts. They have an everyone-plays, no-cut policy. Other teams have no cuts, but they have tryouts as a way to divide the players into balanced teams or to have an A and a B team. Other teams have cuts, which require tryouts.

If your team has tryouts and you're in charge of running them, I suggest the following:

Be organized. Plan every minute so tryouts will proceed in an orderly manner. When a gym is filled with kids, the proceedings can quickly slide into chaos if you're not prepared.

Two days are better than one. If you anticipate that no more than eighteen players will try out, one tryout session should be enough. However, if you expect more than that, have a two-session tryout. After the first day, you and the other coaches have time to reflect on who's a sure thing, who's not, and who's in the middle. On the second day, you can focus on a smaller number of players, the kids you need more time to evaluate. Also, some players, after seeing the competition in the first session, might decide to withdraw.

Get lots of assistants and tell them the plan. Even if only fifteen girls try out, you'll need help. You can't run efficient *stations* (see page 22) without having an assistant at each one. Get enough help so you don't have to worry about the details. You'll want time to walk around and watch kids doing different things. If you don't have enough help, you'll be stuck at one basket, and you won't see what you need to see to make good judgments.

Maximize use of the baskets. When six players are on the court doing a drill while twenty-five other kids are on the sidelines, the latter will quickly turn into a distraction. If you plan right, you and the assistants shouldn't have to spend much time on crowd control. Use every basket available. If you have only two, use the middle of the floor for evaluating passing, dribbling, and shooting form.

It's a tryout, not a clinic. Some coaches approach tryouts as they would a clinic. They take a lot of time to teach skills. At practice, this is great, but at tryouts, this takes time away from evaluating players. Use tryouts for their intended purpose.

Test fundamentals. You want to see how well each player dribbles, passes, and shoots, and how good she is at defense and rebounding. This sounds obvious, but you'd be surprised at how many tryouts don't provide a good opportunity to evaluate each player in terms of the basics. Some try-

Ask the Coach

Question: We have fourteen players trying out. I'd like to have no more than thirteen on my team, but I feel bad having to cut only one player. Any advice?

Answer: That's a tough thing for the one girl who is cut. I'd keep all of them. One more player won't make any difference. Who knows—maybe the player you would have cut will become one of your best players down the road.

outs are nothing but scrimmages. Scrimmages are a good way to see the top 10 percent and the bottom 10 percent of the players. However, the majority of the players fall into a large gray area. Evaluating the kids in this middle group isn't easy. Specific skill-oriented drills should be part of tryouts. This is where stations come into play.

Scrimmage 3-on-3. The best scrimmage format is 3-on-3, either half court or full court, with the players playing man-to-man defense. This makes it hard for any player to "hide." With 5-on-5 and even 4-on-4 scrimmages, some players fade into the background. They don't touch the ball on offense, and the player they're guarding might not touch the ball. With 3-on-3, each player is out in the open for the coaches to see.

What to Do in Tryouts: The Details

Now that you know the big picture, let's get into the details. Assuming you have 2 hours per session, break down the time you have along these lines:

> Introductory talk and warm-ups: 15 minutes
>
> Conditioning drills: 15 minutes
>
> Water break: 5 minutes (use the time to set up stations)
>
> Station work: 25 minutes (assumes 4 to 6 baskets)
>
> 1-on-1 rotation: 20 minutes (start at last station basket)
>
> Water break: 5 minutes (use the time to split players into teams)
>
> 3-on-3-on-3 scrimmaging: 20 minutes
>
> 5-on-5-on-5 scrimmaging: 15 minutes

Introductory talk. Your comments should be brief and enthusiastic. Introduce yourself and the other coaches or assistants. Explain what will happen over the next 2 hours, how the teams will be chosen, and how cuts, if any, will be made. Reassure the players that they're not alone—everyone is anxious at tryouts. Tell them you're glad they're there. Encourage them to do their best.

Warm-ups. The purpose of warming up is to prepare the muscles for vigorous exercise. Have the players start off with moderately paced drills. Players should never start off at full speed. Not warming up properly can result in pulled muscles.

Here are some good warm-up drills to use at tryouts (see Part Two):

Full-Court Dribbling (Drill 17)

Full-Court Passing (Drill 21)

Two-Line Layups (Drill 43)

Full-Court Layups (Drill 44)

Slide the Court (Drill 48)

After the players warm up, they should stretch for 2 to 3 minutes. Stretching before warming up is another way to cause injuries.

Conditioning drills. Conditioning drills will tell you which players are in shape. Make the conditioning part of tryouts strenuous (but not grueling). If someone doesn't like working hard, you want to find out now, not at practice. You might even have a few players decide not to return for the second day of tryouts because basketball is "too much work." Don't try to convince them otherwise. It's best for them and the team that they drop out.

Here are some good conditioning drills to use (see Part Two):

Victory Sprints (Drill 5)

Full-Court Passing (Drill 21)

Three-Man Weave (Drill 24)

Outlet Layups (Drill 61)

The best conditioning drills involve the ball. Not only are the players getting in shape, but they're working on a skill at the same time.

Station work. Split the players into groups and send each group to a different *station*, a basket where they'll work on a specific skill. Before tryouts begin, assign an assistant to each station with instructions on how to run that station.

After 3 to 4 minutes, the players rotate to the next station. When each group has been at each station, the players remain at the last basket to begin 1-on-1 rotation (see below).

Station work is an excellent way to evaluate fundamental skills, particularly shooting. The following are ideally suited for station work:

Free throws (best out of 10)

Elbow jump shots (number taken in 30 seconds)

Right-hand layups (number taken in 30 seconds)

Left-hand layups (number taken 30 seconds)

1-on-1 rotation. Number the baskets 1 to 6. Explain to the players they're going to play 1-on-1 until the offensive player scores or the defender gets the ball. Players line up at the top of the circle. The first player in line is the defender, and the second player is the offensive player. The offensive player has to *check the ball*—that is, hand it to the defender before starting. After each contest, the winner goes to the next higher basket (e.g., from basket 3 to basket 4), and the loser goes to the next lower basket (e.g., from basket 3 to basket 2). The next two players in line become the next offensive and defensive players. When a player at the highest numbered basket (basket 6) wins, she keeps playing there. When a player at the lowest numbered basket (basket 1) loses, she keeps playing there.

What happens is that the best players rotate to baskets 5 and 6, the less-skilled players rotate to baskets 1 and 2, and the average players stay in the middle baskets. This drill is excellent for seeing who can drive and score, who can defend, and who blocks out. It allows you to watch each player match skills against players of varying abilities. It also separates players on its own, which lets the players see where they stand in comparison to the rest of the girls.

Scrimmaging. As noted earlier, watching players scrimmage 3-on-3 is an excellent way to evaluate them. To make it continuous and involve more players, have three teams of three players do Three-on-Three-on-Three (Drill 65). You can see who is aggressive, who is confident with the ball, who passes well, who dribbles with her head up, who knows how to protect the ball, who attacks the boards, who dives on the floor, and so on.

Though 5-on-5 scrimmages aren't as informative, you can still learn a lot. Watch who shows leadership, who works hard to get open, who sets screens, who runs the fast break, who helps on defense, and who hustles.

When you run scrimmages, try to match teams against teams with comparable abilities. Watching a trio of experienced players pound a trio of beginners doesn't provide any useful information. After the 1-on-1 rotation, you'll have a good idea about the relative skills of the players. An easy way to split into comparable teams after the 1-on-1 rotation is to say, "OK, everyone at baskets 1 to 3, go to this half of the court. Everyone at baskets 4 to 6 go to that half of the court."

Evaluating Players Evaluating players isn't easy. Before tryouts begin, print out a one-page tryout evaluation sheet that covers everything you think is important (see the sample in the Appendix). Make enough copies so you and your assistants each have one for each player. During tryouts, make notes. If you don't write down your observations as they occur, you won't remember them later. Though it's inconvenient to pause during the action to jot something down, it'll be worth it when it's time to make decisions.

There's another good reason to use an evaluation sheet. The upset parent of a player who doesn't make the team may call to ask why his or her daughter was cut. It helps if you can say, "In the shooting drills, she made only 18 percent of her shots and didn't make any layups." This helps dispel the notion that you were haphazard in your decisions. It also gives the correct impression that you're an organized, professional coach who takes the responsibility seriously.

How to Handle Cutting Players Your team or league may have a no-cut rule. If so, you'll be spared one thing no coach enjoys—cutting players.

There's no easy way to tell a young player she's not good enough to make the team, but some ways of giving her the bad news are better than others. I don't like the practice of posting a list in the hall for everyone to see. There's no reason to create a situation where three players are jumping for joy, shouting "We made it!" while another player walks up to find out her name is missing. Posting a list might be convenient for you, but it's not fair to put a kid through the embarrassment.

Write two simple form letters, one starting with "Congratulations for making the team" and the other starting with "We're sorry to tell you we didn't choose you for the team" (see the sample end-of-tryouts letter in the Appendix). Write a handwritten note on each letter, put each girl's letter in an envelope, and seal it. At the end of the last session, after thanking the players for trying out, give each player her envelope (make sure each girl gets the *right* envelope). Tell them not to open them until they're home.

It's best if you can add a brief evaluation section at the bottom of the letters, as in the sample. Regardless of whether you keep or cut a player, make the evaluation positive. Rate each player's skills, as well as the intangibles (such as hustle and court savvy).

Starting Up

First Meeting with Players and Parents

After the team is chosen, meet with the players and parents. Before or after the first practice is a good time. Require that at least one parent (or guardian) attend. Limit your comments to no more than 5 to 7 minutes, along these lines:

1. Introduce yourself and your assistants. There's no need for extensive personal histories.

2. Tell them how excited you are to coach the team. Show enthusiasm and positive energy.

3. Describe your coaching philosophy—a brief description of what you value as a coach, such as hard work, hustle, punctuality, defense.

4. Talk about playing time. Will it be equal, as mandated by the league or school, or based on performance? This is the time to mention the consequences of missing practice.

5. Go over the schedule and when and where the team will practice.

6. Ask for money, if appropriate. Some teams provide uniforms for free, but others don't. In the latter case, part of your job is being the toll collector.

7. Ask for volunteers. Besides one or two assistant coaches, you'll need a team parent (to set up the phone/e-mail tree, coordinate the team party, help with the paperwork, keep track of uniforms, and so on), stat

keeper, scorebook keeper, and clock keeper for games. Welcome anyone who volunteers!

8. Pass out the sheet with the team rules and expectations (see the sample player-parent handout in the Appendix), the game schedule, and the medical permission and release form *at the end* of the meeting. If you do it at the beginning, the parents will read as you speak and won't listen to you.

9. Ask for questions. If someone seems to have a concern, tell him or her you'll be glad to talk after the meeting.

10. Thank everyone for coming. Remind everyone that your phone numbers are on the handout.

Communicating with the Team

If you aren't organized, you'll have problems from the start. Coaching involves managing details that are often moving targets. The schedule established at the start of a season rarely stays the same. Snow cancellations and unexpected gym unavailability ("Hey, how come no one told us this was cheerleader practice?") are part of the season.

In the pre-Internet age, the traditional way coaches communicated with their teams was by bulletin board or a phone tree. A phone tree still

Calling All Volunteers!

If you have parents who want to be part of the team but don't want to help out on the court, by all means use their enthusiasm to take over the administrative details. There are routine but important administrative aspects to running a team that could be taken over by a manager or several committed parents:

Phone/E-Mail Tree

Instead of having to call every player whenever there's a change in the schedule, have one parent arrange a phone or e-mail tree. You can call one designated person, who then initiates a reliable chain of communication, or you can e-mail everyone simultaneously.

Practice Transportation

A designated parent can be in charge of carpooling by checking that each player has a ride to practice and home again. Though many families won't need this help, the safety net it provides for those who do is reassuring. This parent should make certain that all players are picked up from practice before he or she leaves.

Fund-Raisers

Getting all of the necessary equipment can be somewhat expensive. Having team dinners, organizing fund drives, and arranging other fund-raising events are projects that an administrative parent can organize, with some of the duties delegated to other team parents as well.

Snack Duties

A small, nutritious snack after practices or a trip to the ice cream stand after a game can be a helpful boost or well-deserved reward for your young players. A parent can be in charge of this service or can create a rotating schedule of parents who would be interested in helping. This is a fun and highly satisfying way that parents can be involved with the team.

works today, but many coaches have switched to an e-mail list. Determine what works best for your team. If you use an e-mail list, include the e-mail addresses for the players and their parents.

Team Rules and Expectations

Every team needs rules. Without clear guidelines, your players won't know what's right and what's wrong. Before the season, establish a set of team rules. At the first practice, discuss them briefly with your players. With my teams, we have a one-page contract that I ask the players to sign. You don't need to go to that extent, but you should write down the main rules and expectations that you list in the handout for the meeting with players and parents. Explaining the rules before the season gets underway avoids confusion and misunderstandings later on.

Enforce the rules. If you let one player slide by with a minor infraction, the other players will think they can also slide by. It's easier to be tough in the beginning of the season than it is to turn tough as the season goes on. Make the rules and penalties clear at the beginning, stick by them the first time and every time, and you'll avoid problems with players and parents.

Team rules and expectations should include the following areas:

Tardiness and absences. It's an unusual team that doesn't have players who are sometimes late or absent. Determine your parameters before the first practice. When someone is late or absent, find out why. There's a difference between an excused absence (the player had a dentist's appointment) and an unexcused absence (the player went skiing). Decide how you'll view it when a player misses a practice because she's playing travel soccer or club volleyball. My view is that if a player takes up a spot on the team, she's committing to being there all the time (barring legitimate reasons). Only you can decide what's right for you. If your team is low on players, you might have no choice but to live with players not showing up because of other sports. Let common sense guide you. You can't hold a player accountable for being late when her parent is her only transportation.

Disruptive behavior. Some players have loud personalities. They like to talk and socialize. Players who are new to being on a sports team sometimes need time to learn what's expected. Be patient with these players. They mean well and will soon learn when to be quiet and when to talk. Every now and then, you'll have a player who is disruptive because she's not accustomed to respecting adults. These players become problems if you don't enforce the rules. You can't allow anyone to disrupt practice. Coaching is a benevolent dictatorship. How to enforce the rules is up to you.

Poor sportsmanship. Fighting, cursing, insulting the referee, and other similar behavior can't be allowed on your basketball team. Everyone deserves a second chance, but if a player displays poor sportsmanship the second time, she shouldn't stay on the team.

Expectations. List the expectations regarding effort, hustle, and attitude. Also list expectations having to do with practicalities, such as bringing a water bottle to practice.

The handout you prepare should be no longer than a page, should present information clearly, and should be full of enthusiasm. See the sample in the Appendix.

Disciplining players. When a player breaks a minor rule, such as being late for practice, make her run five laps or do ten pushups. If she breaks the rule a second time, add two more laps or another ten pushups and have a brief talk with her. Tell her you expect that she won't break the rule again, but if she does, it will hurt her playing time. If she breaks the rule a third time, take away playing time. Talk to her and a parent or guardian in private about the situation. Listen carefully to be sure you know all the facts. Make sure there are no extenuating circumstances. In an extreme case, when it's obvious a player is a constant disruption, you'll have to dismiss the player from the team.

Assistants and Other Helpers

It's difficult to coach a basketball team without help. There are too many tasks for one person to handle. One of your priorities at the player-parent meeting is to find people for these roles:

Assistant coaches. Without one or two assistant coaches, too much of your practices will be spent in crowd management. With assistants, the players receive more individual attention, stand around less, and can work on multiple skills at the same time. In games, assistants can provide important information and advice. It's simple—using assistants makes you a better coach. See the sidebar on page 28 for more on choosing assistants.

Stat keeper. You'll need someone at the games to keep accurate stats regarding fouls, rebounds, assists, steals, turnovers, and blocks. If you need to train this person, do so in advance of the first game. Have him or her get experience by keeping stats in a practice scrimmage. See the sample stat sheet in the Appendix.

Scorebook keeper. You'll need someone to keep the team's scorebook at the scorers' table. When your team is the home team, your scorebook is the official scorebook for the game. Choose someone who knows how to keep the book or, lacking that, make sure the person learns what to do. (See the sample scorebook sheet in the Appendix.)

Clock keeper. In most middle school leagues, the home team is responsible for *keeping the clock*—starting and stopping the clock, as well as adding points on the scoreboard. The clock keeper has few things to worry about, but if he or she makes a mistake in a close game, the coaches and fans can get testy. Make sure your clock keeper knows what to do.

Team parent. As mentioned above, a team parent can take a lot of the organizational details off you (such as preparing the phone/e-mail tree, calling other parents, setting up a team pizza party, collecting medical

Ask the Coach

Question: A friend has volunteered to be an assistant, but she doesn't know a thing about basketball. What should I do?

Answer: Is she enthusiastic? Is she smart? Is she organized? Is she willing to learn? Does she relate well to kids? If you answered "yes" to these questions, she should make a good assistant. It would be better to have someone like her as an assistant than someone who might know more about basketball but lacks those important qualities. Don't limit your search for people to assist you. They can come from a wide group of people—parents, siblings, older players, friends, and so on.

Question: How much should I involve my assistants in running drills?

Answer: A lot. Inexperienced coaches underutilize their assistants, letting them stand on the sidelines all practice long and failing to consult them during games. This is like having no assistants. Tell your assistants you value their input and advice. As part of each practice, split your players into groups (guards/posts or first stringers/second stringers). Send one group with your assistants to the other half of the court. This way, your players get more individual coaching. In games, confer with your assistants. Listen to them with an open mind. When addressing the team, ask your assistants if they have anything to add. If you use your assistants wisely, you'll be a better coach, and they'll jump at the chance to help you next year.

Question: When I volunteered to coach the team, a dad offered to help. Since I don't know much about basketball, I said yes. Now, two weeks into the season, the dad is taking over. He interrupts me in front of the kids and has them do drills he and I didn't talk about. I see the kids looking from me to him, not knowing whom to listen to. What should I do?

Answer: No wonder the kids are confused. Change the situation before it worsens. Take the dad aside and tell him that a ship can have only one captain, and a team can have only one head coach. Remind him that the team has a head coach, that you're happy to have his help, but only if he's willing to be an assistant. Hopefully, he's just an eager dad who'll understand he overstepped his limits. If he gets huffy and tells you he's quitting, thank him for his time and walk away before he changes his mind.

Question: I have someone I'd like to have keep the scorebook, but she's reluctant because she has no experience. Is keeping the scorebook complicated?

Answer: Not at all. Every scorebook includes a sample game in the front of it. Look at it with your scorekeeper and make sure you both understand how to record what happens during the game. Have her practice during a scrimmage. Most people not only learn how to keep the book accurately, they come to enjoy it.

release forms and money for shoes). A good team parent helps the team run smoothly.

How to Run Effective Practices

Practices are the backbone of your season. Good practices guarantee that your players and team will improve. Bad practices guarantee that your team won't be prepared to compete in games. Coaches are fond of saying "You play like you practice." I've found that to be true.

What makes a practice a "good" practice? First, you made every minute count. Second, the players worked hard and were focused. And third, the players improved a little bit.

But, you might say, some players improved only a little bit, and some didn't improve at all. Many basketball skills, like shooting and ball handling, take a long time to develop. If your players improve a little bit every practice, over the course of the season the little bits will add up to a lot of improvement. Here are the principles for running good practices:

Plan, plan, plan. Start with a master practice plan for the season, a comprehensive list of all the things you want your players to learn (see the Appendix for a sample). Then, make weekly practice plans for the first several weeks. If you want your players to learn zone defense, in what week do you want to introduce it? When do you want to teach them about breaking full-court presses? What about a sidelines play? Ideally, you'd teach them everything they need to know before the first game. In reality, this is impossible. You may have only four practices before the first game, or maybe only two. Make a daily practice plan for each practice leading up to the first game (see a sample in the Appendix). Choose priorities, recognizing that the most you can do is prepare your players partway. Plan everything down to the last minute.

Start on time. Starting practice on time sets the proper tone for how you intend to run the team. When you don't start on time, you send the message that punctuality isn't important. The players and parents will assume that it's acceptable to be late and will arrive late as a routine. By the end of the season, you won't be able to count on anyone to show up on time. You can easily avoid this problem—start on time the first time and every time.

Keep things moving. Practices are like games in that they have a certain amount of momentum. If the players waste time moving from one drill to the next, momentum will be lost. If you let things slow down, the girls will start to chatter. Keep up the pace. There is plenty of time before and after practice for socializing.

Game speed and intensity. Insist that your players practice at game speed and game intensity. Playing with intensity isn't natural for most girls. They don't want to embarrass their teammates, so they play passively when they play against them. Explain that it's their job to practice as hard as they can, that their teammates are counting on them. If your players don't practice at game speed and game intensity, they'll be unprepared to play in games.

Conditioning. Running laps or sprints will condition your team, but why not work on basketball at the same time? Have your players get in shape while working on skills. Many drills, like Three-Man Weave (Drill 24), are perfect conditioners. As the players' endurance improves, so do their passing skills.

Stick to the daily plan. When your players are struggling with a drill, it's tempting to stick with it until they get it right. Resist this temptation. Beyond a certain point, the drill will provide diminishing returns. The players will get more frustrated, which will make it harder for them to do it right. Some days, things won't work they way you planned it, no matter how hard the players try or how much you repeat yourself. That's the nature of coaching. When the time for a drill is up, move on to the next drill.

When introducing a new skill or drill, demonstrate it. If you can't demonstrate it, have an assistant or an experienced player demonstrate it. Seeing skills and drills demonstrated is a key part of learning.

Plan for maximum player participation. This is the same principle you used in tryouts. The fewer players you have on the sidelines watching, the better. Stations are a great way to have everyone working. This is when assistant coaches are so important. Split your team into groups for part of every practice. Working with a small number of players is when some of your most effective coaching is done.

Repetition. When you introduce a new concept or drill, repeat it over the next several practices. Everything you teach needs to be revisited throughout the season. Repetitions are how players learn.

Adjust your daily plans as you go. After each game, analyze what your team did well and what it did poorly (see the sample game sheet in the Appendix). Adjust your next practices to address the areas needing improvement. If the team had too many turnovers, work on passing under pressure. If the team missed a bunch of layups, work on layup drills. If the team ran out of gas in the second half, work on conditioning.

Fundamentals. I've already emphasized how important it is to practice fundamentals, but it bears repeating. Half of every practice should be devoted to fundamentals. As the season proceeds, you can cut this time back a little. Game experience is important, but how much you practice fundamentals is the basis for how much your players improve.

Develop a list of core practice elements. Over the years, I've developed a list of a dozen elements of the game I want my team to practice every day

Coach Hatchell's Twelve Core Practice Elements

1. Dribbling
2. Shooting
3. Free throws
4. Passing
5. Rebounding
6. Half-court offense
7. Press offense
8. Fast break (this will work on conditioning)
9. Individual defense
10. Half-court defense
11. Transition defense
12. Controlled scrimmage

Ask the Coach

Question: How much time should I give to each drill?

Answer: I plan my practices in segments of time, for example, 5 minutes for this drill and 8 minutes for the next one. I also include time for team talks and water breaks. When I've listed everything I want the team to work on, I total the segments. If needed, I cut a drill out or add a drill.

(see the sidebar opposite). In my daily practice plans, I include at least one drill that addresses each element. I may choose a different drill the next day, but I make sure to cover the element.

Vary the pace. Mix up the drills. After a slow-paced drill like shooting free throws, schedule a fast-paced drill like Outlet Layups (Drill 61). After your team has run Three-on-Three-on-Three (Drill 65), shooting free throws is a perfect follow-up.

Scrimmages. Other than in the first few practices of the season, my teams scrimmage at almost every practice. These aren't free-for-all scrimmages without rules, but *controlled scrimmages*, with restrictions. For example, in one scrimmage the teams might play only a 2-3 zone, so we can practice our zone offense. In another, the shots can come from only our post players, which forces the perimeter players to work on passing to the post. We also routinely practice *time and score* situations, where I stipulate that a certain amount of time is left in the game and that the team is ahead or behind by so many points. Make your scrimmages as gamelike as possible.

Keep a practice notebook. This is an essential practice tool. After practice ends, write down what worked well and what didn't. This will come in handy later in the season and even next year. As you become more experienced, your practices will become more effective.

CHAPTER 2

Teaching the Fundamentals

Warming Up

There's a proper sequence for warming up your players at the beginning of every practice. They first should go half-speed for 5 minutes. Jogging up and back, full-court dribbling, defensive slides, and Two-Line Layups (Drill 43) all serve this purpose well.

Players should then stretch for 2 to 3 minutes. Have someone lead them through the proper sequence. At the beginning of the season, you or an assistant coach should lead the warm-up, but once they know what to do, have a player lead warm-ups. Every player on the team should lead at least once during the season.

Stretches should work on the major muscle groups: legs (quads, hamstrings, calves), arms (biceps, triceps), and torso (back, laterals, glutes). After this, the players are ready for intense physical activity. Right after stretching is a great time for a high-energy drill such as Full-Court Layups (Drill 44) or Outlet Layups (Drill 61).

When a player's in the ready stance, she's ready to play basketball!

Footwork

Ready stance. Basketball is a game of running and jumping, with sudden changes of speed and direction. Players need to play in the *ready stance*, a body position that prepares them for these movements. In the ready stance, a player's knees are bent, her feet are shoulder-width apart, and her hands are up and out.

Her back is straight, and her head is centered over her body. She's balanced, ready to spring into action, not needing a split second to lower her body before running, sliding, or jumping. The ready stance is the foundation of all basketball movements.

Jump stops. One of the first skills your players should learn is how to come to a complete stop with or without the ball, with their body under control and balanced. The footwork involved in a *two-foot jump stop* is simple. Imagine a player running. When she plants her right foot, she decides she wants to stop. As she steps with her left foot, her right foot also leaves the floor. She makes a little hop and lands on the floor with both feet. To stop her momentum, she lands with feet wide, knees bent, arms out, her back upright. She's in the ready stance, ready to make the next move.

The same footwork applies in coming to a jump stop with the ball. As the player makes the little hop, she holds the ball securely in both hands so it doesn't jar loose when her feet hit the floor.

To practice jump stops, the players line up on the baseline, facing the court. Have them step with their left foot, take a little hop, and land on both feet. Then, have them jog down the court and come to a jump stop every time you yell "Stop!" Once they can do this, have them sprint down the court, again stopping on your instruction. When they've mastered this, have them practice jump stops with a ball. At first, they shouldn't dribble, but just carry the ball. When they have the footwork down, add the dribble. Last, have them dribble as fast as they can and come to a jump stop.

A dribbler coming to a jump stop.

Pivoting

The next step is learning how to pivot. *Pivoting* is a movement in which a player uses one foot as a point upon which to spin her body. This is the *pivot foot*. Her other foot moves forward or backward as she pivots. As long as the player doesn't lift the ball of her foot off the floor or drag it, she's allowed to pivot until she decides what to do with the ball (remember—she must get rid of it within 5 seconds).

Line up your players, each with a ball, and have them get in the ready stance. Tell them to raise the heel of their right foot and rotate on the ball of the foot, maintaining contact with the floor, as their heel swings from side to side.

Next, have them step forward with their left foot, again spinning on the ball of their right foot. As they step, their left arm and shoulder should also swing forward. This is a *forward pivot*. Have them step their left foot

A player pivots to protect the ball.

The triple threat position. This player is ready to dribble, pass, or shoot.

back to where they started, again maintaining contact with the floor with the ball of their right foot. This is a *reverse pivot*. Once players are comfortable with pivoting on their right foot, have them practice pivoting on their left foot.

Pivoting with the ball is a fundamental skill. When a player has the ball and can no longer dribble, pivoting is the only way she can protect the ball from a defender who's trying to steal it.

Start with the players in the ready stance with a ball held securely with both hands off their right hip (left hip for left-handed players). This is called the *triple threat position*, because from this position the players are ready to dribble, pass, or shoot. Their elbows should be away from the body. Keeping the ball on the hip protects it from defenders.

Have the players *rip the ball*, or sweep it across their body so it's held off the opposite hip. This motion should be forceful to prevent the defender from grabbing the ball. Have the players hold the ball over their right shoulder and rip it low so it ends up low by their left foot. Have them repeat the movement, ripping the ball from their left shoulder to their right foot.

Combine ripping the ball with pivoting. The goal is to rip the ball, elbows out, combining forward pivots with reverse pivots, so the defenders can't touch the ball without fouling.

Practicing pivoting and protecting the ball. Split the team into pairs, each pair with a ball. Have one player practice pivoting and ripping the ball while the other player tries to snatch it away. The offensive player should keep her elbows out as she moves the ball. The sight of a flying elbow will make the defender think twice about being too close. Teach pivoting players to swing their bodies as they swing their elbows. If a player swings only her elbows and makes contact, that's a foul. A player should never swing her elbows with the intent to hit another player.

When the player brings the ball across her body, she rips it through.

Catching the Ball

Before a player can learn to dribble, pass, or shoot, she must learn how to catch the ball. This is one of the most important and under-emphasized fundamentals.

When a player is open for a pass, she should *call for the ball* by showing the passer the palms of her hands as a target (see photo next page). Her hands should be chest high, fingers open and pointing to the ceiling. Receivers who play with their hands held low often fumble the ball because they can't raise their hands in time. If the passer doesn't see her, the player should call her name.

When the pass is in the air, the player should *jump to the pass*, making a two-foot jump stop as the ball hits her hands. This gives her the choice of using either foot as a pivot foot. She shouldn't jump high off the ground in an exaggerated manner. A low two-foot hop is all that's needed.

When catching, the player keeps her eye on the ball until it's in her hands.

A player calls for the ball, letting her teammates know she's open.

Once the player catches the ball, she should *square up* (or *face up*) to the basket by pivoting toward the basket and facing it in the triple threat position. Now she can see if anyone is open near the basket, and she's ready to dribble, pass, or shoot.

Dribbling

There is no more important fundamental skill to learn in basketball than dribbling. When a player learns to dribble under pressure with either hand and with her head up, her confidence increases, and her whole game improves. Your team should practice dribbling every practice.

Dribble with a purpose. Young players tend to dribble right away after they catch the ball, without knowing where they're going or why they're going there. We've all seen young players dribble around the perimeter, back and forth, their head down, while the other players stand around watching. The dribble is a valuable skill, but aimless dribbling is a liability.

Players should dribble for one of only three reasons:

- to drive toward the basket
- to create a better passing angle
- to get out of trouble

Dribbling concepts. The two most important concepts to teach about dribbling are:

Fingertip control. The dribbler must use the pads and tips of her fingers, not the palm of her hand, to push the ball down. This gives her much better control over where the ball goes.

Head up. The dribbler must keep her head up, with her eyes focused on what's happening on the court. Dribblers who can't look up won't see open teammates, will miss good chances to take the ball to the basket, and will dribble into trouble. Defenders notice when a player can't dribble without watching the ball, and they'll attack her. This makes it harder for the dribbler to stay poised and do something positive with the ball. A dribbler who can't keep her head and eyes up has no *court vision.*

The natural tendency of the beginning dribbler is to stare at the ball.

She wants to make sure it bounces back to her hand. This is normal but should be discouraged from the start. During dribbling drills, have your players look up, even if the balls bounce off their feet over and over. This is a necessary part of the learning process. They'll soon tire of fetching the ball, which will force them to learn how to dribble sooner.

A good way for players to practice dribbling is to look at the ceiling.

Basic Dribble Moves

The three dribbles you should teach your players are the control dribble, the speed dribble, and the crossover dribble.

The *control dribble* is used when a defender is guarding the dribbler closely. Protection of the ball is the top priority. The dribbler positions her body and the ball in a *body-body-ball* line, that is, she keeps her body between the other player's body and the ball. She holds her nondribbling arm as a shield and dribbles low for control. Players must learn how to protect the ball under pressure when dribbling with either hand, always looking up to see the court.

The *speed dribble* is used to advance the ball quickly from one end of the court to the other, typically while running a fast break. In a speed dribble, the player pushes the ball ahead of her, bouncing it so it's chest high, keeping it in front of her as she runs. She can use either hand, or if no defender is pressuring her, she can alternate hands. This allows her to run up the court faster. She should take several steps between each dribble. The fewer dribbles she makes, the faster she'll get to the basket.

This player is using a control dribble. Note how she keeps her body between the ball and the defender.

In the *crossover dribble*, the player dribbles in front of her body, changing her dribbling hand (see photos next page). The crossover is used to protect the ball from the defender's reach, to create a better angle for a pass, or to change directions for a drive to the basket. The technique is simple. Assume the dribbler approaches a defender dribbling with her right hand. She suddenly makes a short, hard dribble in front of her feet, bringing the ball over to her left hand. The dribbler keeps the ball below her knees so the defender can't steal or deflect the ball as it passes in front of the dribbler's body.

The crossover dribble. The player starts dribbling with her right hand (left). Then she suddenly dribbles low and hard in front of her feet (middle). The ball is now in her left hand, and the crossover is complete (right).

Make sure you devote enough practice time to dribbling with the weak hand. Players who can dribble with only one hand limit their value on offense.

Passing

The best way to beat the defense is with a good pass. Good passes keep the ball out of the hands of the opponent, make the defense work hard, and create excellent opportunities for easy shots. Passing drills should be a standard part of every practice.

Passing stance. The stance for passing the ball is similar to the ready stance. The player is low, with knees bent and her feet shoulder-width apart for good balance.

Fingertips. The ball should be on the player's fingertips, which gives her more ability to control the ball.

Ball fakes. A *ball fake* (or *pass fake*) occurs when a player pretends to throw a pass in one direction, causing the defender to react, and then sets up an easy pass in the other direction. Coaches like to say "Fake a pass to make a pass."

Ball fakes should be varied. A player who fakes the same way every time becomes predictable. She should fake low and pass high; fake left and pass right; fake high and make a bounce pass. For a fake to be believable, the player must look in the direction of the fake.

Types of Passes

There are several basic passes to learn, each useful in a different situation. Passes should be hard and crisp. Defenders love soft, lazy passes because they make for easy steals and easy layups. Bad passes account for the majority of turnovers in basketball.

In the *chest pass*, the player uses two hands to pass the ball from her chest to her teammate's chest. The player steps to her target and pushes the ball from her chest, snapping her wrists so her thumbs point to the floor in her follow-through.

A *bounce pass* is a pass that bounces once on the floor before reaching the intended player. The passing motion is the same as the motion used in the chest pass. The player steps to the target, and her thumbs point to the floor after the pass. Bounce passes shouldn't be attempted when the passer is a long way from the receiver.

The *push pass* (see top photo next page) can be an *air pass* (one that goes straight to the target) or a bounce pass. It's a one-handed pass that begins near the passer's shoulder and is often set up by a ball fake. Players should learn to make sharp push passes with their weak hand, not just with their strong hand.

The *curl pass* is the best pass to use when passing from the wing to a player in the low post.

First, the fake (left) . . . then the pass (below).

For a bounce pass, the passer aims for a spot on the floor two-thirds of the distance to her teammate.

Push pass. Snap that ball!

The passer takes a big step across the defender's body, extends her arm, and wraps the ball around the defender's leg. Younger players will need time to learn this pass, but it's a fundamental pass that needs to be taught early. Players should practice making curl passes with both hands.

To make an *overhead pass*, the player raises the ball above her head with both hands, brings it slightly behind her head, steps toward her team-mate, and brings her arms forward at the same time, snapping her wrists as she releases the ball. When used to pass the ball from one side of the court

Curl pass. The passer wraps the ball around the defender.

to the other over the top of a zone defense, it's called a *skip pass*. When used by a rebounder to start a fast break, it's called an *outlet pass*.

The *baseball pass*, a pass thrown like a baseball, is used to throw the ball a long way. However, because your players' hands will be small, this pass will be awkward for most of them. Unless your players are advanced, don't spend time on this pass.

A quick outlet pass starts the fast break (left).

Baseball pass (right). The player aims her nonthrowing hand at the target.

Shooting

Kids love to shoot. Unfortunately, many do so with bad habits. All the time they spend shooting only reinforces those habits. One of your most important jobs as a youth or middle school coach is to teach good shooting habits and form.

Practice and patience. No basketball player has ever completely mastered shooting. Michael Jordan made less than 50 percent of his field goals, though he worked on his shooting every day.

There are no shortcuts to becoming a good shooter. Your players can only become good shooters by practicing sound mechanics over and over. Encourage your players not to get discouraged when they miss.

Balance and stance. The foundation of a good shot begins with the proper stance and good balance. The first thing to teach your players is the *ready-to-shoot* position.

Set up one line of players on the free throw line extended and another line 6 feet behind it. Each player should have a ball, but they begin with the ball on the floor. With their eyes on the basket, players get in the ready position. They should stagger their feet slightly by placing their lead foot 6 inches ahead of their other foot. For right-handed players, the lead foot is their right foot (see photo next page). For left-handed players, it's the left foot. Check that your players' shoulders line up perpendicular to an imaginary line running from the basket to them.

Once your players are in the proper stance, ask them to look at their feet and memorize how they look. Anytime they shoot, no matter where

Foot position for right-handed shooters.

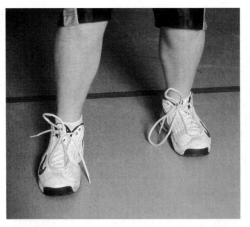

they are in relation to the basket, their feet and shoulders should line up the same way. This is called *squaring up*. Many shooters forget to square up during the excitement of the moment. They shoot before their feet are set or with their bodies leaning to one side. As a result, they miss hard shots and make easy shots hard. It takes only a split second to square up. Doing so increases the odds that the shot will go in.

Hand, arm, and elbow. Once your players are in the ready-to-shoot position (still without a ball), have them stretch their shooting hand out toward the basket, palm pointing to the ceiling. Have them bend their elbow, bring their hand back next to their shoulder, and twist their palm so that it is again faceup. In this position, the players should look like waiters carrying invisible trays of food to the table. The upper part of their shooting arm (the shoulder to the elbow) should be parallel to the floor, and the bottom part of the arm (the elbow to the wrist) should be perpendicular to the floor, creating a 90-degree angle. When viewed from the side, their arms should form a backward L shape.

Make sure the players' elbows point to the floor. One of the common shooting flaws is a *chicken wing*, where the shooter's elbow sticks out from her body at an awkward angle.

Lifting the shot. Once your players are in the ready-to-shoot position, have them think of what happens next as *lifting* the shot. Tell them to pretend that they have a release button under their shooting elbow, and that when you say "Go," to imagine that someone presses the button, causing them to release the shot. The first few times, have your players do this in slow motion.

Once a shooter's arm is cocked and ready, the shooter must do several things at the same time. As her legs straighten, her elbow rises and her arm extends. As the arm reaches full extension, her wrist snaps and her fingers direct the ball toward the basket. Her index and middle fingers provide most of the force. If her wrist snaps properly, the ball should have a noticeable backspin as it travels through the air. Backspin sometimes creates a *shooter's roll*, where the ball bounces around on the rim softly before dropping through.

Follow-through. After the ball leaves her hand, the shooter's elbow should be at eyebrow level, and her arm should be at a 60-degree angle to the floor. Her arm should be straight, her wrist bent, and her fingers should *wave goodbye to the ball* by pointing to the basket.

Tell your players to hold their follow-through for a few moments after

they shoot to make sure they've done it properly. Poor follow-through is a common cause of missed shots.

Eyes. The shooter's eyes should never leave the target throughout the shot. Too many young players watch the ball after it leaves their hand, which distorts their follow-through.

Grip. Have your players pick up the ball and go through the ready-to-shoot sequence. When they have the ball cocked and ready by their shoulder, have them freeze. Check the position of each player's shooting hand. The fingers should be spread apart, and the pads of the fingers should cradle the ball. The ball shouldn't touch the palm of the hand. No matter how small a player's hand is, you should see space between the ball and their palm.

Guide hand. Now it's time to add the nonshooting hand, called the *guide hand* (this is a misnomer—the guide hand only steadies the ball). Players stand with the ball cradled by their face and their body in the ready-to-

The shooter makes an L with her shooting arm (left).

The shooter extends her arm in a lifting motion, not a pushing motion (middle).

A good follow-through is a thing of beauty (right)!

Notice the space between the shooter's palm and the ball.

Note the guide hand before the shot (left). Note the guide hand after the shot (right).

This player is perfecting her shooting form.

shoot position, and they raise their guide hand to the side of the ball, not the top of the ball or in front of it. The fingers of the guide hand should point straight to the ceiling.

A common shooting flaw of younger players is that their guide hand follows their shooting hand as the shot is released. This is a leftover habit from when they were smaller and had to shoot two-handed to reach the basket. Players whose guide hand influences their shots shoot the ball inconsistently. Inconsistent shooting means poor shooting.

A good way to break this habit is to have the player practice shooting with her guide hand held behind her back. She can lie on her back on the floor and practice this as well (see Floor Follow-Through, Drill 31).

Types of Shooting

Form shooting. Now your players are ready for form shooting. Pair each player with another player and have them use one ball to shoot to each other as they stand 8 to 10 feet apart. Another way to work on form shooting is to have each player shoot against a wall. Form shooting should be part of every practice.

Players should aim at the *backboard* when they shoot from a 45-degree angle to the basket, unless they are beyond 12 feet from the basket.

When the ball hits the backboard before hitting the rim, it's called a *bank shot*.

Why use the backboard? First, it's easier for a shooter to aim at a visible surface than it is to aim at an invisible plane stretching from the rim. Second, a bank shot has a bigger margin for error than a shot bouncing off the rim. Third, using the backboard requires the shooter to aim the ball higher than if she were only trying to get the ball over the lip of the rim. This helps players shoot against taller defenders.

When using the backboard, the ball should hit the surface on the way down, not on the way up. The shooter should aim at the top near corner of the square painted on the backboard The square is white on clear fiberglass backboards and black on white backboards.

Part of being a good shooter is having good *shot selection*, that is, knowing what's a *good shot* (a high-percent-

Remind your players that the backboard is shooter-friendly.

age shot) and what's a *bad shot* (a low-percentage shot). With my teams, I consider a good shot one that the player can make at least 60 percent of the time in practice (unguarded). Decide on your own parameters, based on the skill of your players. If your team has beginners, a good shot might be any open shot taken inside the free throw line.

Teach your players about good shot selection by emphasizing it in scrimmages. Award a point when a player takes a good shot and deduct a point when she takes a bad shot. It won't be long before the players learn the difference.

3-point shots. Few girls aged 6 to 12 have the arm strength to shoot a 3-point shot with good form. Unless your players are advanced, don't practice shooting 3-point shots.

Layups. Beginners have a hard time shooting layups, particularly with their weak hand, but layups are the easiest shot in basketball and must be learned.

Layups are soft shots. If the ball is put up too hard off the backboard, it will bounce off the front rim every time. Players should shoot the ball with an open hand, with the palm facing the backboard, and aim for the top corner of the square. As players approach the basket, they should extend the body up, not forward (see top photo next page). Too many players run under the basket at full speed and fling the ball up, hoping it will go in. These shots rarely go in, and the players take themselves out of position for the rebound.

The layup is easy when the shooter extends her body to the basket.

You can't see it, but there's a string attached from this player's knee to her elbow!

When teaching layups, break it down into several steps. Start with right-hand layups for righties and left-hand layups for lefties.

Have your players line up along the free throw line extended, each with a ball. Tell them to imagine that one end of a string is tied to their shooting elbow and the other end is tied to their knee on the shooting side. When the players extend their arm, the string pulls their knee up at the same time. Have them shoot the ball in the air so it lands a few feet ahead.

Move the player line to the right-side block (left-side block for lefties). Have the players shoot from the block, taking no steps or dribbles and focusing on the shooting arm and the knee working together. Their eyes should focus on the upper corner of the square as they shoot.

Back the line up a step. Right-handed players should now step with their left foot and shoot. Back the line to the second hash mark. Tell your players to memorize the sequence by saying it out loud: "left-right-left-and-up." Have them take three steps (left foot first) and shoot the layup. Once they can do this fairly well, have them go faster.

Lastly, have them dribble once with their right hand as they take the steps. Once they learn the footwork, start them farther back. Have them approach the basket faster. It won't be long before most of them are shooting layups like veterans.

It's essential to work on weak-hand layups at an early age. Too many high school players can't make left-hand layups because they didn't learn how to shoot them when they were in middle school.

Foul shooting. A player awarded a free throw should first step to the line and set her feet so they're spaced equally on both sides on the line's midpoint. She should take a deep breath to relax (this is especially important if the player is breathing heavily from running). Next, she should go through a brief sequence of motion, a *free throw routine* that prepares her for the shot. Every player has her own routine—some players dribble a few times, some spin the ball, some whisper special words. It doesn't matter what the routine is as long as each player does the same thing every time.

Once players develop a routine, shooting a free throw is exactly like shooting a field goal, except that there's

Players should take their time at the free throw line. They have 10 seconds in which to shoot.

no defender. All the principles of sound shooting form apply (balance, grip, eyes on the target, lifting the shot, follow-through).

Work on shooting free throws every practice. A made free throw late in the game can mean the difference in who wins.

Shooting drills. Every time your players work on shooting, they should begin with form shooting to hone their mechanics. Too many players (and coaches) think that elementary drills like form shooting should be done only at the beginning of the season. With my teams, we never stop working on fundamentals. We practice form shooting several times a week.

For some excellent shooting drills, see Drills 31–46 in Part Two.

Rebounding

A *rebound* is a shot that misses the basket and bounces off the backboard or the rim onto the court. An *offensive rebound* occurs when a player misses at the opponent's basket. A *defensive rebound* occurs when a player's opponent misses at the basket the player is defending.

When a shot misses the basket entirely, it's not a rebound. It's a pass (often followed by fans of the nonshooting team chanting "Air ball, air ball"). When a rebound bounces on the court, the ball is still in play. When a rebound lands on the baseline or outside of it, the ball is out of play. The team that didn't shoot inbounds the ball.

Every team needs good rebounders.

There is no more critical aspect in basketball than rebounding. A rebound can mean as much as a 6-point swing in the score. When your team snags a defensive rebound, the other team loses the chance to score 2 or 3 points, and your team now has the chance to score 2 or 3 points.

That's not to say your team can't win a game in spite of being outrebounded—maybe your team shot the lights out or the other team couldn't make a shot—but no team at any level will succeed over the course of a season without good rebounding.

What does it take for a player to be a good rebounder? A little technique and a lot of desire. A player doesn't need to be the best athlete or the tallest player to be the team's best rebounder. This is good news for young players. Convince them how important rebounding is, that anyone who works hard at it can be good at it, and you'll see some of your players develop into good rebounders.

Rebounding is one of the pillars of good basketball. Devote part of every practice to it.

Types of Rebounding

Defensive rebounding. The rebounding technique used in defending your basket is called *blocking out* or *boxing out*. The defender's goal is to position herself between the offensive player and the basket. If the rebound bounces in her direction, she's in perfect position to grab it.

To block out, the defender faces the offensive player, no more than 3 feet away, and does a reverse pivot so her back and rear make contact with the player. She holds her arms wide so the offensive player can't get around her. Her hands are above her elbows, her feet are wide apart, and her body is low and balanced. With this strong base, she can keep even a

bigger, stronger player *on
her back* for the second
needed for the ball to come
off the basket.

The defender uses her
legs to push the offensive
player away from the basket.
This allows her to maintain
contact with the player and
creates a bigger area where
she can get the ball. If the
player tries to get around
her, the defender takes
short, choppy steps to maintain contact and keep her
on her back.

When the ball comes
off the basket, the defender
goes after it, her hands up
and fingers wide. She jumps

When the defender gets the
other player on her back,
the defender has won the
rebounding battle.

and extends her arms, trying to time the jump so she catches the ball at the
peak of her jump. After the defender catches the ball, she *chins it*—brings it
down to just below her chin with both hands, keeping her elbows wide.

Last, the defender pivots away from the offensive player (who is now a
defender) and any other opposing players, and she looks up to see if she can

Once the ball comes off the
backboard or the rim, the
rebounder goes for it (left).
Chinning the ball protects it
(right).

No one's taking the ball away from this rebounder!

throw an outlet pass. If she can't, she passes to the point guard.

Offensive rebounding. A player who is a good offensive rebounder is valuable. Offensive rebounders score easy baskets and are often fouled in the process.

When a player grabs an offensive rebound, she should keep the ball over her head and immediately jump back up and shoot it (this is called a *putback* shot). Inexperienced players make the mistake of bringing the rebound down to their waist, which gives the defenders a chance to knock the ball away or cause a held ball. Tell your offensive rebounders not to hesitate when they grab the ball. Keep it over their head and go back up strong!

After the player grabs an offensive rebound, she should keep the ball high and go back up to shoot.

Getting Open: Moves without the Ball

A player can't score if she doesn't have the ball, and she can't get the ball if she can't get open. Players who can't get open are nonfactors on offense. It's like playing 4 against 5. Teach your players the V-cut-and-swim move and the backdoor cut.

The *V-cut-and-swim move* is used when a player wants to get open on the perimeter. The move begins when the player cuts toward the basket, drawing her defender with her. When she nears the block area, she grabs the defender's arm with her hand (the hand closest to the ball), swings her outside arm (the one away from the ball) over the top of the defender's head and shoulders in a swimming motion, and cuts back out to the perimeter. The path she takes should form a V, not an I—she shouldn't cut back along the same path. It's better to cut too close to the ball than to cut too far from it.

Teach your players to change speeds when getting open. When drawing the defender toward the basket, the player can walk down. When she's ready, she plants her inside foot, swims over the top so her head and shoulders are ahead of the defender, and sprints toward the ball. Players who play at the same speed are easy to defend.

The *backdoor cut* is the opposite of a V-cut. The player takes her defender away from the basket and then cuts back to the basket. Before using this move, the player should signal to her teammate with the ball that she's about to make a backdoor cut by raising her fist.

The player takes one or two steps away from the basket, holding her hand up as if she's about to receive a pass (the player with the ball should fake a pass). The player then plants her outside foot and cuts hard to the basket, going behind the defender for an easy pass and layup. Backdoor cuts are good weapons against teams that play aggressive man-to-man defense.

Moves with the Ball

Once a player receives the ball on the perimeter, she must decide what to do from the triple threat position. This is where shot fakes and jab steps come in.

The first move to learn is the *shot fake*. The player pretends to shoot the ball so the defender straightens up to contest the shot. The player fakes by raising her shoulders, head, and the ball, though the ball shouldn't come above her chin. She looks at the basket so the fake will be convincing. Shot fakes (and ball fakes) shouldn't be rushed. If the player fakes too fast, the defender doesn't have time to react to the fake.

If the defender reacts to the fake by rising up out of her defensive stance, the player should drive by her.

The next moves to teach are *jab steps*. A jab step is a short (6 to 8 inches) out-and-back step to see what the defender will do. Right-handed players should jab with their right foot, and left-handed players should jab

The swim move before the V-cut.

First, the shot fake (left) . . . then the drive (right).

with their left. If the defender does nothing, the player should immediately take a long step in the same direction with the same foot and drive by. She should make the first dribble ahead of her lead foot, not beside it. This is called the *jab-and-go move*.

If the defender reacts to the jab step by backing up in the direction of the jab, the player should simultaneously bring the ball and her lead foot across the defender's body and drive by the defender on the other side. The first dribble should be with her other hand. This is called the *jab-and-cross move*. As with the jab-and-go, the first step after the jab-and-cross should be long and explosive.

Screens

A *screen* (or a *pick*) occurs when a player uses her body as a temporary wall to block a teammate's defender. There are two basic screens: on-ball screens and off-ball screens.

The *on-ball screen* (or *ball screen*) is set on a defender guarding the player with the ball. The purpose is to create an open driving lane or an uncontested shot. The *off-ball screen* (or *player screen*) is set on a defender guarding a player without the ball. The purpose is to help the player get open for a pass.

Screens also have other names, depending on where they're set. A *cross screen* occurs when a player comes across the lane to screen for a player on the other side. Cross screens can be from block to block or from elbow to elbow.

A *down screen* occurs when a player comes down from the perimeter to screen for a player in the low post area, and an *up screen* occurs when the

In this on-ball screen the player in the white T-shirt without the ball has set a screen on the dribbler's defender. The screener's defender has stepped out to stop the drive (left). Off-ball screen (right).

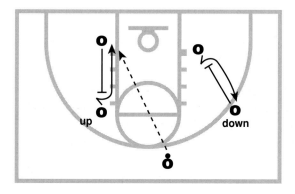

reverse happens, that is, a player comes up from the low post area to screen for a player on the perimeter.

Setting a screen. To set a screen, the player runs at the defender and comes to a two-foot jump stop next to her, making slight contact with the defender. When a player screens behind the defender where the defender can't see her, the rules say the screen must be a foot away. The screener's feet should be wide, with her knees bent, so she's ready for a collision if the defender runs into her. Her arms should be held in an X across her chest to protect herself and to cushion the physical contact. She can't hold her arms out from her body. That's a foul.

As she runs to set the screen, she should let her teammate know she's screening for the teammate by calling the player's name or raising a fist. Once she sets the screen, she can't move until her teammate has used the screen, that is, until she has either cut or dribbled by. Many young screeners are so eager, they run after the defender, trying to screen her, which is a foul called a *moving pick*. Even if the screener leans a little to one side or takes a small step, it's a foul.

After the screen has been used, the screener should *open up to the ball* by turning and facing the teammate with the ball. To open up properly, she should imagine that she has a piece of Velcro on her shoulder, as does her teammate. As her teammate dribbles or cuts by, rubbing shoulders, the Velcro pulls the screener in the correct direction.

Defenders are so focused on the dribbler or the cutter, they often forget about the screener. This often leaves screeners open for a pass. If your players are advanced, teach them how to run a *pick-and-roll*. After the dribbler cuts by her, the screener opens up to the ball and *rolls* (moves) to the basket. If the dribbler doesn't have a good drive available, she should look to see if the screener is open. Much of the time, the screener is wide open. The pick-and-roll is a good tactic against a team that plays man-to-man defense.

Using a screen. If a player doesn't use the screen a teammate set for her, she's missed a good opportunity to get open. There are two principles to remember when using a screen:

Wait for the screen. If a player doesn't wait, her teammate's efforts will be wasted, and the player won't get open. Worse, when her teammate sees the defender moving before she gets there, she might commit a moving pick violation. It's better to be too late to use a screen than to be too early.

Rub the screener's shoulder. As the player cuts or dribbles by the screener, make sure her shoulder rubs the screener's shoulder. This leaves no space for the defender to follow the player through.

Post Play

Which players will make good post players? The saying in basketball is, "You can't coach height." Coaches at all levels like to have tall players in hopes the players will be good *post players* (or *posts*), that is, good rebounders and inside scorers. However, not every tall player is a good post. Height helps when trying to grab a rebound, but it's only one ingredient. Desire, aggressiveness, and technique are more important. Your best rebounders may or may not be your tallest girls, but they understand the importance of blocking out and going hard after every missed shot.

Tall girls often develop physical coordination more slowly than short girls. It takes time before they can run without being awkward or gangly. Their hand-eye coordination isn't developed yet. Be extra patient with your tall players, as they can only do so much of what you ask.

Players who don't like physical contact won't like being a center or a power forward. As you decide who will play these positions, look for players who think nothing of diving on the floor for a loose ball and players who are comfortable using their bodies to push people around.

Most youth and middle school coaches don't teach *post moves*, that is, back-to-the-basket scoring moves. Given the limited practice time, this is understandable. However, if you have an advanced post player and the time, teach her how to post up and how to shoot a turn-around jump shot.

In order to receive the ball in the low post, post players must *post up*—use the proper footwork and stance to get open for a pass.

Posting up is like blocking out a rebounder. The player faces the defender no more than 3 feet away, steps toward her with either foot and makes a reverse pivot with her arms out. The post stays low, with her feet and arms wide, so she'll have the leverage to hold the defender in place. She must make contact with the defender or the defender will slide around to deflect the pass. The post's objective is to keep the defender behind her and face the passer, her hands up, ready for the ball.

Once the post player catches the ball, she chins it and takes a second to look over her shoulder to see what the defender is doing. Most post players don't pause, and as a result, they make poor decisions about what to do.

If the defender tries to get around the post to prevent the pass, the post should use short, choppy steps to maintain contact and keep the defender on her back. The rules prohibit a player from hooking her arm around a defender and holding her, but the post is allowed to keep her arms stiff and wide.

Many players post up too far under the basket or along the baseline, where they have a poor angle for a shot. Players should post up above the block, outside the lane to avoid a 3-second call.

In posting up, the lower the player is, the stronger she is.

To shoot a *turn-around jump shot*, the post player fakes one way and pivots the other. She can fake to the middle of the lane and pivot toward the baseline, or she can fake toward the baseline and pivot toward the middle of the lane. The key to a believable fake is looking where she's faking and leaning in that direction. As the defender shifts position to cover the anticipated move, the post quickly pivots in the opposite direction, bringing the ball over her head as she does. Jump shots from the low post must be released higher than regular jump shots so the defender is less likely to block them.

Handling Traps

A *trap* occurs when two defenders guard an offensive player by forming a V with their bodies and preventing her from dribbling.

The best way for a dribbler to handle traps is to avoid them. This gets back to the importance of the dribbler keeping her head up so she can see what the defense is doing. If the dribbler finds herself in a trap, she shouldn't panic. She should pivot forcefully to protect the ball and wait for a teammate to get open for a pass. She should use ball fakes. She can also *split the*

Good defense means working hard. Here, the defender goes after a loose ball.

trap, a technique in which she steps between the defenders with her nonpivot foot to make the pass.

Your players should practice being trapped so they'll know what to do if it happens in games.

Individual Defensive Skills

In teaching individual defensive skills, emphasize the following concepts:

Defense wins games. Good defense (including rebounding) is the foundation for winning games. You can't count on your offense—sometimes shots go in, and sometimes they don't—but you can rely on your defense to keep the other team from scoring too many points. If you make it hard for the other team to score, your team can be competitive in every game. Defense isn't based on skill. It's based on effort and intensity. If you can convince your team to buy into that concept, you'll be on your way to having a good defensive team.

Anyone can play good defense. A player doesn't need to have great athletic ability or experience to be a good defender. Any player on your team can learn to play good defense. It starts with her making it a goal and working hard at it.

The defense never rests. Playing defense requires nonstop energy. The instant a team relaxes on defense, the offense gets an easy shot. Your players should never stop working hard on defense. It won't be long before the offense loses patience, and someone forces a bad pass or shoots a bad shot.

Don't give up layups. The number one shot you want your defense to prevent is the layup, the highest-percentage shot in the game. Your defenders should be ready to leave their assigned man or zone to stop the other team from shooting layups.

Know where the ball and your man are at all times. Many players focus on the player they're guarding. They follow their man all over the court and lose track of the ball. This results in not being in position to help their teammates when the defense breaks down. Other players focus so much on the ball that they lose sight of their man. This results in their man getting open for an easy pass or score. For good reason, coaches say, "See ball, see man."

Keep moving. Good defense is about being in the right position. A defender shouldn't stand in one spot for more than an instant. Every time the ball moves or her man moves, she should adjust her position.

Play defense with your feet. When players get tired, they start standing around, playing defense with their arms and hands. Defenders who don't

When the ball is in the lane, the defenders drop down to protect the basket.

move their feet can't keep up with the offense. They wave their arms as dribblers go by, often committing a reaching foul. They arrive too late to get in front of a player driving for a layup, often committing a blocking foul. If you see a player not moving her feet on defense, take her out for a rest.

Drop to the basket. When the offense is able to move the ball close to the basket, all five defenders should *drop to the basket* by coming into the lane to help prevent an easy shot. They should try to force the offense to pass the ball back to the perimeter, where it's less likely to hurt them.

Teach man-to-man principles. Even if you decide to play zone defense, it's important to teach man-to-man principles because they apply to all defenses. If you don't, your players will play zone passively. They'll think they're guarding a space on the floor instead of guarding players who are in that space, they won't understand the difference between guarding someone

---

"Defensive" Talk

There are five offensive players on the court, each doing something at the same time, and it's impossible for one player to see what they're all doing. Good teams communicate on defense. Teach your players to shout the following when playing defense:

"Shot!" alerts everyone to block out for the rebound.

"Cutter!" tells everyone that someone is trying to get open in the lane for a pass.

"Ball!" tells the team that a player is guarding the player with the ball.

"Help!" alerts everyone that the player with the ball has dribbled by the defender, and someone needs to stop her.

near the ball and someone far from the ball, and they won't know how to help when a teammate gets in trouble. In other words, without learning man-to-man principles, your players won't know how to play good team defense.

Types of Individual Defense

There are three types of individual defense, depending on the relative position of the ball and the player whom the defender is guarding: on-ball defense, denial defense, and help-side defense.

Before understanding how to teach each of these defenses, you must understand the difference between the *ball-side* half of the court and the *help-side* half. Imagine a line that runs from one basket to the other. When the ball is in one half of the court, that half is the ball side, and the other half is the help side.

Defenders must understand this concept to know where to be and what stance to use.

On-ball defense. On-ball defense occurs when a defender guards the player with the ball.

The defender positions herself at an arm's-length distance from the offensive player, between her and the basket. Her stance is like the *ready stance*—her body is low, her feet are wide apart, her knees are bent, her back is straight, and her hands are out, palms up. One foot should be ahead of the other by 6 to 8 inches, depending on which way she wants to force the player with the ball. If she wants the player to dribble to her right, her left foot is ahead. If she wants to force the player to dribble to her left, her right foot is ahead. Most of the time, she'll want to force the dribbler to the dribbler's left, because most players are right-handed and don't dribble as well with their left hand.

When the player dribbles, the defender stays between her and the basket using a *step-slide* motion. If the dribbler goes to the defender's right, the defender pushes off with her left foot, steps with her right foot, and slides her left foot quickly so she's in the defensive on-ball stance again. As she step-slides, her arms stay wide, ready to prevent a pass. She shouldn't

Ball side and help side.

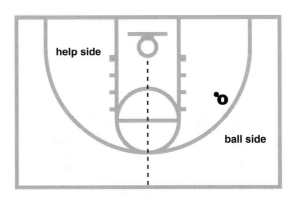

cross her feet. If the dribbler starts to drive by her, she should get out of the on-ball stance, turn, sprint ahead of the dribbler, and resume the defensive stance when she's again between the player and the basket.

If the dribbler backs up, the defender should use an *advance step*. The lead foot steps toward the player and the back foot slides forward. In a *retreat step*, the back foot steps toward the basket and the lead foot slides in place. When the defender wants to switch from her lead foot to the other foot, she uses a *swing step*. She makes a reverse pivot by swinging her lead foot back until it's 6 to 8 inches behind the new lead foot. When the dribbler makes a crossover dribble, the defender uses the swing step to stay in good on-ball position.

This on-ball defender is in perfect position.

If the dribbler is careless about protecting the ball, the defender tries to poke it away. If the dribbler picks up her dribble, the defender gets out of her low stance (she doesn't have to worry about the drive anymore), steps right up to the player, and moves her hands to try to prevent a pass. Her objective is to force the player to make a bad pass.

Advance, reverse, and swing steps.

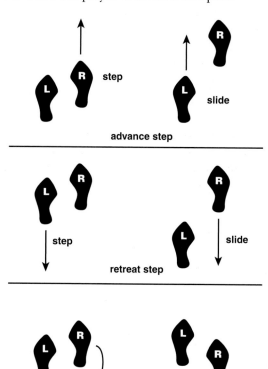

When guarding the shooter, the defender gets her hand up to contest the shot (left). When the defender tries to block a shot, she keeps her hands straight up to avoid a foul (right).

If the offensive player picks up her dribble to shoot, the defender should raise her lead hand to discourage the shot and distract the shooter.

On-ball defenders should avoid the temptation to reach across the player's body or slap at the ball. When she's forced the player to pick up her dribble, the last thing she wants to do is to rescue the offensive player by fouling her.

Denial defense. When a defender guards a player who's one pass away from the ball, she plays *denial defense*—she *denies* the player from receiving a pass.

Assume the ball is at the top of the 3-point circle and the defender is guarding a player on the left wing, as viewed from the basket. The defender stands in a *closed stance* to the ball—her back is to the ball handler, and she stands no farther than 6 feet away from her man. She's low, her knees are

Denial defense.

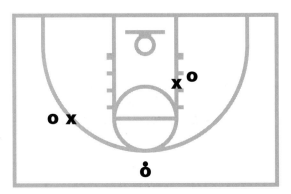

bent, and her nearest hand and foot are in the *passing lane*, an imaginary line from the player she's guarding to the ball. She looks over her shoulder at the passer, not at her man, whom she can see with her peripheral vision.

If the pass is thrown, the defender bats it away with her denial hand. If the player cuts to the ball, the defender moves her feet to stay in between the player and the ball in the denial stance. If the player cuts toward or away from the basket, the defender stays with her, using a step-slide motion, keeping her hand up, and staying low the whole time.

Help-side defense. Help-side defense occurs when the defender guards a player two passes away from the ball and on the help-side half of the court.

The help-side stance is different than the on-ball stance and the denial stance. The defender stands in an open stance, with her feet apart, her body balanced, her knees bent, and her arms out. She

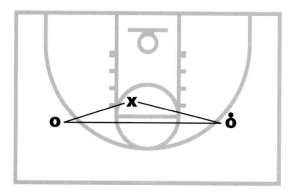

See man, see ball. This help-side defender points to both (above). Help-side defense triangle (left).

Ask the Coach

Question: Just like you said, I taught my help-side post to stand in the center of the lane when the ball is at the opposite wing. The trouble is, when she steps toward the dribbler to stop her from coming into the paint, she leaves her man, and the dribbler makes an easy pass for a wide-open shot. How do I prevent this?

Answer: This is where *help-side defense* comes into play. When someone goes over to stop a dribbler driving to the basket, the other defenders should sprint back into the lane not only to guard the dribbler but also to prevent the dribbler from passing to an open player. High school teams learn what are called *defensive rotations* (rules of movement to use in help situations), but most youth and middle school players aren't advanced enough to learn these concepts. For now, teach your players to drop to the basket when someone drives. This will cover most situations.

points one hand at her man and the other at the ball. She stands where she can easily see the ball and her man by turning her head. The spot where she's standing forms a shallow-angle triangle with the other two points. She should face the other basket, ready to move when either her man or the ball moves.

When a defender is on the help side, her primary responsibility is to make sure the player with the ball can't drive and shoot a layup. If the player with the ball is above the free throw line extended, the help-side defender stands with one foot in the lane. If the player with the ball is below the free throw line extended, the help-side defender stands in the middle of the lane, straddling the line between the ball side and the help side. The defender is deep enough in the lane so that if the player with the ball suddenly dribbles to the basket, the defender can stop her from entering the lane.

Two players set a trap, making it hard for the ball handler to see her teammates.

Trapping A trap occurs when two defenders guard the player with the ball by forming a V with their bodies. Their feet and shoulders make a 90-degree angle, and their hands are held above their shoulders to discourage passes and avoid fouling.

Several spots on the court are ideal for trapping

Best trapping areas.

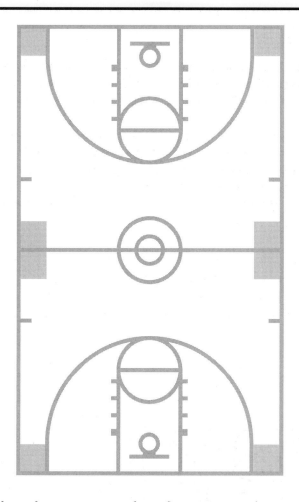

because the boundaries prevent a player from escaping the trap: the corners formed by the baselines and sidelines, and the corners formed by the sidelines and the midcourt line. If your team has quick, aggressive players, consider making traps a part of your defense. If the other team has weak ball handlers, have your players trap them.

C H A P T E R   3

Teaching Team Offense

Principles of Team Offense

New coaches are often unsure what offensive strategies to choose. In this chapter, I present a few simple offenses and a few advanced offenses. If you're interested in considering other options, you'll find them available in the dozens of books and tapes you can buy. The key is to choose offenses that suit the strengths and weaknesses of your team. It's more important to run an offense well than to select a particular offense.

It takes time to learn and hone any offense, so keep things simple. Resist the temptation to add things just because this or that famous coach runs it. You're coaching young girls, not college or NBA players.

Given the age of your players, the most you should teach is two man-to-man offenses, two zone offenses (one for *one-guard fronts*, one for *two-guard fronts*, which are explained on pages 71 and 74–76), two plays designed to get the ball to your best players, one press offense, one sideline play, and four baseline out-of-bounds plays. Teaching more than this is overkill.

The following principles apply to any offense:

Spacing. In youth games, it isn't unusual to see ten players standing within 10 feet of the ball. This clogs the court and makes it hard for the offense to get a good shot. Good offensive spacing spreads out the defense, so one defender can't guard more than one player. The ideal passing distance between offensive players is 12 to 15 feet. If the distance is shorter, there are too many defend-

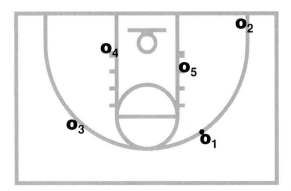

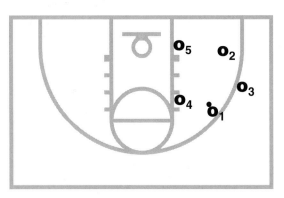

Good offensive spacing (top). Bad offensive spacing (bottom).

ers in a small area. If the distance is longer, the ball is in the air too long, allowing a good defender the chance for a steal.

Player movement. Young players tend to stand around watching the dribbler. An offensive player who doesn't move is easy to guard. Good offensive players don't stand still unless they're wide open. The four players without the ball should move constantly, cutting to the ball, cutting to an open spot, or moving to screen. Just as it's important to dribble with a purpose, it's important for the players without the ball to move with a purpose.

Control. Young players tend to play too fast. They dribble out of control, they pass before the receiver is open, they cut to the ball before the passer is ready, they shoot before they're squared up, and they run into the game from the sideline before the referee signals for them to come in. This is all part of youthful exuberance. Good players play fast, but they don't rush.

Shot selection. Young players tend to take bad shots. Teach your players the difference between good shots and bad shots. They shouldn't take shots they can't make, nor should they shoot from far out when a teammate is open near the basket.

Ball reversal. Ball reversal occurs when a team passes the ball from one side of the court to the other. Too many teams only play offense in the right side of the court. This is because most point guards are right-handed. As soon as the point guard dribbles to the top of the circle, she passes to the right wing or dribbles to the right wing. This becomes predictable, and defenders start cheating over to that side. Playing only in part of the court is bad offense. Ball reversal is good offense. It forces the defense to make big movements in position, which creates openings. Practice ball reversal when you practice half-court offense. Insist that your point guard initiate the offense by going to the left some of the time.

O offensive player

O' player with ball

X defensive player

A number beside an **X** or an **O** is the position of that player. For example, **X₅** is the defensive center and **O₂** is the offensive shooting guard.

————————▶ player movement

- - - - - - - -▶ pass

∿∿∿∿∿▶ dribble movement

————————┤ player screen or trap

Diagram key.

Ball reversal through the point (left). Ball reversal through the high post (right).

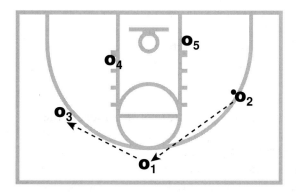

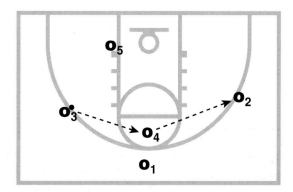

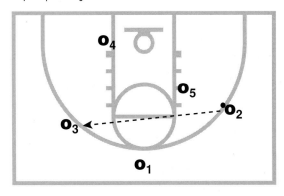

Ball reversal using a skip pass.

Offensive balance. Teams that always shoot from outside or teams that always pass to one player are one-dimensional and easy to defend. If you have a star player, don't fall into the trap of being a *one-man team*. One-man teams struggle because the defense knows exactly where to put their best defenders, and the other offensive players tend to stand around watching the star. Have a special play geared to your star, but make sure everyone on the floor touches the ball on offense. Make sure the ball goes to the post players as well as to the perimeter players.

Fast-break opportunities. The easiest way to score is on the *fast break*, when your players beat the other team down the court for a layup. Even if you don't have fast players, your team should practice fast breaks. When one of your players gets a defensive rebound or steals the ball, she should immediately look up the court, and her teammates should sprint for the other basket (how to run the fast break is covered on pages 76–79).

Safety. Regardless of what offense your team is using, at least one player should be at the top of the circle to serve as a *safety*, whose job is to sprint back and stop the other team from scoring on a fast break. If you're playing against a team that's good at the fast break, particularly if their players run faster than yours, designate two players to be safeties.

Half-Court Offenses

Half-court offenses fall into two general categories: continuity offenses and set plays.

A *continuity offense* is a sequence of player and ball movement that repeats itself until a good shot is created. There's no shot clock in youth and middle school games, so a continuity offense is an excellent offense for your team. Once your players learn it, you won't have to issue instructions from the bench. All that's needed is patience and execution until a good shot opens up. Another advantage of continuity offenses is that they provide scoring chances for all five players. This makes it hard for a defense to focus on your best players.

A *set play* is a sequence of player and ball movement that has an end. If a set play doesn't result in a shot, the offense must *reset*, that is, the players must go back to a specific alignment to run another play.

Teach two continuity offenses, one for man-to-man defense and one for zone defense, and two set plays that you can call from the bench as needed. If you coach advanced players, you can teach other offensive sets, but I can't emphasize this enough—don't overload your players with too many plays.

If you're interested in learning about the many styles of offense out there, you'll find lots of other books and videos on the subject. You can tweak them to fit the players on your team, or you can make up an offense of your own.

Keep the following in mind as you teach team offense:

1. **Keep offense simple.** This bears repeating—if you're not careful, you'll overwhelm your players with too much information.

2. **Teach offense in stages.** When teaching a new offense, start without defenders. Have your players walk through everything first. When they get it, they can run at half-speed, then at game speed. Only at this point should you introduce defenders. Beginners will find different offenses confusing at first. Some will catch on fast, but others won't. Just as you stress patience to them in running a half-court offense, stress patience to yourself as they learn.

3. **Reinforce fundamentals.** As your players practice offense, reinforce all the fundamentals. Remind them to make ball fakes, to catch the ball in a jump stop, to square up to the basket, to give a target with their hands.

4. **Correct mistakes when they happen.** Stop play when someone makes a mistake. Don't go overboard and stop play every 10 seconds, or they'll never learn the new offense, but correct players when they need correcting. If you wait until later to point out mistakes, the value of the lesson is gone.

Give-and-go (top).

Backdoor play (bottom).

Basic Plays

Over the years, several plays have become standard elements of good offense.

Give-and-go. In the simplest two-man play, the *give-and-go*, a player *gives* (passes) the ball to a teammate, *goes* (cuts) to the basket, and receives the ball back from her teammate. Teach your players to try a give-and-go when they make a pass and their defender turns her head to watch the receiver. The passer should cut between the defender and the ball, calling for the ball.

Backdoor play. In a *backdoor play* a player without the ball makes a backdoor cut (taking a step away from the basket and then making a sudden cut to the basket behind the defender), and the player with the ball passes it to her. Teach your players to make backdoor cuts when their defenders overplay the passing lanes. The player with the ball can help set up the backdoor play by making a good ball fake.

Pick-and-roll. As explained in Chapter 2, in a *pick-and-roll* a screener *picks* (screens) for the player with the ball, who dribbles around the

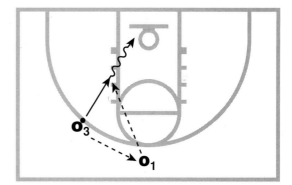

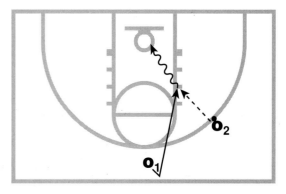

Pick-and-roll.

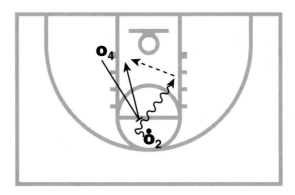

screen, and then the screener *rolls* (cuts) to the basket for a pass or a rebound.

Isolation play. An isolation play is designed to get the ball to a particular player so she can play 1-on-1 against her defender. It's a good play to run when one of your players is better than her defender. It's also a good play to run when a defender is in foul trouble. Isolation plays often involve setting a screen for the designated player.

Man-to-Man Offense: Continuities

Give-and-Go Offense

This simple offense is based on repeated give-and-go action and on players *filling* open spots on the floor by moving to an open spot when they make a cut and don't get the ball. It's best suited to attack man-to-man defenses but also works against zone defenses.

Start this offense with your players in a *3-out, 2-in* formation. Three players start on the perimeter: player 1 at the top of the circle, 2 on the right wing (as viewed from the point), and 3 on the left wing. Player 4 starts on the left block (as viewed from the point), and 5 starts on the right block.

The offense starts when 2 and 3 make V-cuts to get open and 1 passes to one of them. Players 2 and 3 should get open 12 to 15 feet from 1. After passing to 2, player 1 cuts to the basket, looking for the return pass. While 1 makes her cut, 3 *fills the open spot* by replacing 1 at the top. Player 5 posts up.

3-out, 2-in formation (left).

Initial movement in the Give-and-Go Offense (right).

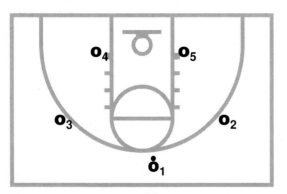

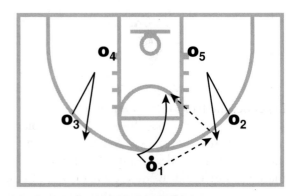

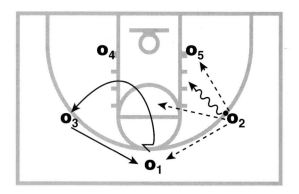

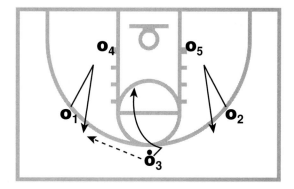

If 1 doesn't receive the pass, she cuts to the opposite wing to fill the open spot. Player 2 has three options: pass to 1, pass to 5 posting up, or drive to the basket, if she has an opening.

If 2 can't do any of these things, she passes to 3 at the top. Now 1 and 2 make V-cuts to get open. If 3 passes to 1, she cuts to the basket, looking for the return pass. Player 2 replaces her at the top. The ball-side post player posts up every time the ball goes to the wing.

The options for player 2 in the Give-and-Go Offense (left). Continuity in the Give-and-Go Offense (right).

Screen-Away Offense

A more advanced continuity offense is to have the perimeter player at the top of the circle *screen away*—pass to one wing player and set a screen for the opposite wing player. This action, combined with a cross screen from post to post, creates good opportunities for players to get open.

The initial formation of the Screen-Away Offense is the same 3-out, 2-in as in the Give-and-Go Offense. The play starts when players 2 and 3 get open on the wing. After 1 passes to 2, she runs at 3's defender and sets a screen. Player 3 waits for her and cuts off the screen. Player 5 sets a cross screen for 4. If your players are good at screening, they'll find themselves open for high-percentage shots.

Screens in the Screen-Away Offense (top). Continuity in the Screen-Away Offense (bottom).

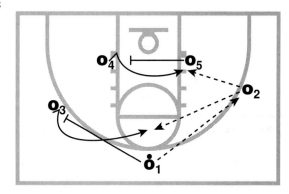

Man-to-Man Offense: Set Plays

Isolation Play

If one of your players is a better player than her defender, run an isolation play, which is designed to get her the ball so she can play 1-on-1.

Start with 1 at the top and the other players in a *double stack* formation. Player 2 will use 5 to screen her man, and 3 will use 4 to screen her man. If 3's defender is the player you want to iso-

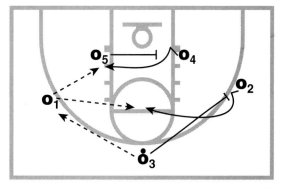

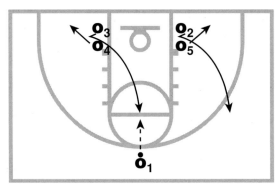

Initial movement in an isolation play (right). The options for player 3 in an isolation play (below).

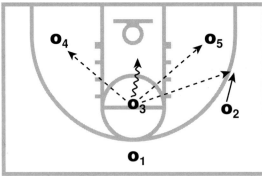

late, 3 will use 4's screen to cut to the free throw line area.

When 1 passes to 3, players 4 and 5 step away to the short corners. This leaves 3 matched up 1-on-1 against her defender. If she drives by her defender, and if player 4's or 5's defender comes over to prevent an easy basket, 3 passes to the open player. She can also pass to 2, who moves to get open on the perimeter.

Wing-Through Play

The Wing-Through Play is designed to get your best shooter the ball for an open shot. If 2 is your best shooter, when 2 V-cuts to get open, 1 passes her the ball. As 2 squares up as if to drive or pass inside, 1 V-cuts so 2 can pass back to her. As 1 passes to 3, player 2 cuts by the screens set by 4 and 5 to the short corner. Before 2's defender can recover, 3 passes to 2 for an open jump shot.

1-4 Low Play

This is an easy play to teach, and it's excellent if your point guard is a good 1-on-1 player. Player 1 begins at the top, and the four other players spread out along the baseline, with 4 and 5 on the blocks and 2 and 3 in the corners.

Player 1 picks a side and drives on her defender. If she dribbles to

Initial movement in the Wing-Through Play (left). Ball reversal in the Wing-Through Play (right).

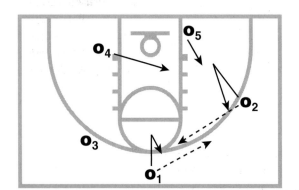

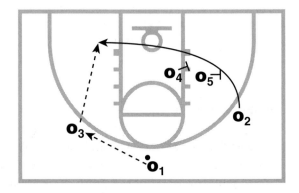

the right, 2 moves to get open on the perimeter, and 3 comes up to replace 1 and become the safety. When 5 sees 1 driving in her direction, she steps out to the short corner. This forces her defender to decide whether to stick with her or to help stop 1's drive. Player 4 steps up the lane above the block, forcing her defender to make the same decision.

Player 1 can shoot, drive the rest of the way, pass to 5 for an easy jump shot, pass to 4 for an easy jump shot, or pass to 2 for a 3-point shot. If she can't do any of these things, she comes to a jump stop, pivots, and passes out to 3.

If 2 and 3 are good 1-on-1 players as well, you can turn the 1-4 Low Play into a continuity offense by having 1 cut to 3's original corner and 5 and 2 relocate to where they started. Now 3 is the new 1-on-1 player.

Zone Offense

In man-to-man defense, each defender guards a player (or *man*). In zone defenses, each defender guards a specific area (her *zone*). When any offensive player comes into that area, with or without the ball, the defender guards her.

Zone defenses are described by using numbers based on the alignment of the defenders as viewed from overhead. The most common zones are the 1-2-2, the 1-3-1, the 2-3, and the 2-1-2. Zones are also described by the number of players positioned at the *top of the zone* (the area closest to midcourt). Zones that have one player at the top (1-2-2 and 1-3-1 zones) have *one-guard fronts*. Zones that have two players at the top (2-3 and 2-1-2 zones) have *two-guard fronts*.

Every zone defense has inherent weaknesses—holes and seams that are vulnerable. The offenses used to play against zones try to exploit these weaknesses. For that reason, it's essential to identify what kind of zone the other team is playing so you know how to attack it (see diagrams next page).

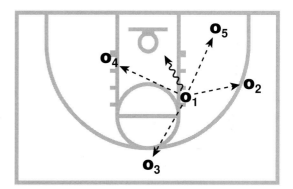

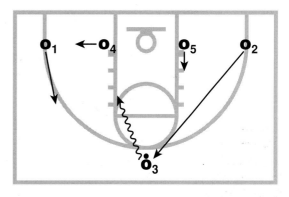

Initial movement in the 1-4 Low Play (top). The options for player 1 in the 1-4 Low Play (middle). Continuity in the 1-4 Low Play (bottom).

Principles of Zone Offense

The following are the principles of attacking any zone defense:

Beat the zone before it sets up. The best offense against a zone is the fast break. When your team gains possession of the ball, your players should push it up the court as fast as possible. There are more opportunities to

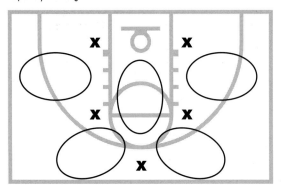

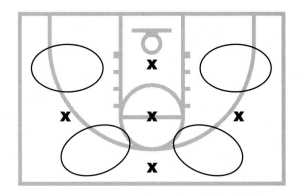

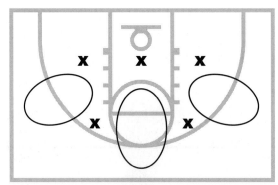

Weaknesses in the 1-2-2 zone (top left). Weaknesses in the 1-3-1 zone (top right). Weaknesses in the 2-3 zone (right). Weaknesses in the 2-1-2 zone (bottom).

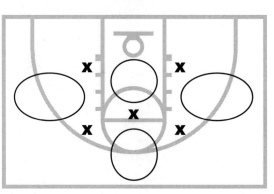

score fast-break baskets against a zone versus man-to-man defense because the defenders in the zone don't have assigned players. This sometimes causes confusion and allows alert offensive players to cut into the lane for an easy score.

Make the zone move. Be patient in attacking the zone. Zone defenders love nothing more than when the point guard makes one pass and the wing takes a long-distance shot. The defenders don't have to move much, and they're in perfect rebounding position. Make the zone defenders work. Pass the ball around. Make them shift position again and again. Take your time until a good shot opens up.

Reverse the ball. *Swing* (pass) the ball from one wing to the other by passing it through the point, through the high post, or use a *skip pass* (a pass from one wing to the other over the top of the zone). Ball reversal forces zone defenders to move rapidly to new positions. As they move, gaps and seams open up for drives and passes.

Attack the seams with the dribble. This is called *dribble penetration*. Anytime one of your perimeter players sees a crack in the zone, she should dribble into it. This draws two defenders to her, making it easy to pass to an open teammate.

Use ball fakes. Zone defenders react to ball fakes, so offensive players should use them to open up passing lanes and driving lanes. Don't just tell your players to use ball fakes. Practice them.

Attack the zone from behind. Zone defenders tend to face the player with the ball and not look behind them. The alert offensive player can take advantage of this by cutting along the baseline looking for an open spot. By the time the defense realizes it, the ball zips by their ears, and the offensive player scores 2 points.

Flash from the help side. Offensive players on the help side should be alert for the chances to *flash* (cut) into empty spots in the zone. Zone defenders often lose track of players outside of their area, particularly away from the ball.

Attack the boards. Offensive rebounding is easier against zone defenses because zone defenders don't have an assigned man to block out. When a shot

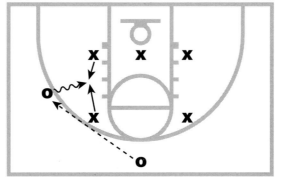

Dribble penetration.

The result of dribble penetration is an open teammate.

Attacking the zone from behind (left).

Flashing from the help side (right).

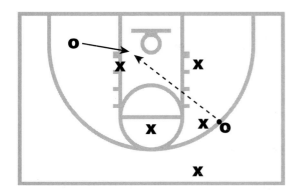

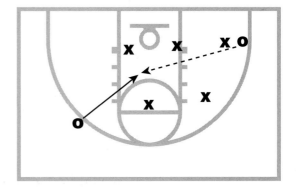

is taken from one side of the court, the offensive players on the help side should cut to the basket for a possible rebound.

Two-Guard Offense

Initial movement in the Two-Guard Offense (top). The options for player 1 in the Two-Guard Offense (middle). The options for player 4 in the Two-Guard Offense (bottom).

Attack zones with one-guard fronts (1-2-2 and 1-3-1) with the Two-Guard Offense. This puts your players where they can attack the gaps in the zone. Position two guards at the top, each to one side of the top zone defender. It's impossible for that defender to cover two players. Position your best passing forward at the free throw line and 3 and 5 each in a short corner.

To begin the offense, 1 dribbles at the gap between the top defender and the elbow defender. When the defenders close in on her, she has several options: she can pass to 2 (who will be open), to 3 (who should be trying to sneak behind the defense), to 4 in the middle, or to 5 posting up.

The primary weakness of the 1-2-2 zone is in the middle, so the player with the ball should always look for chances to pass to player 4. The primary weakness of the 1-3-1 zone is along the baseline, because there is only one defender assigned to the area. Against that zone, the player with the ball should look for chances to pass to the short corners.

When the ball goes to the middle, 4 has several options:

- shoot, if she's open
- pass to 3 or 5, if either is open
- drive, if no one is guarding her when she catches the ball
- pass to the opposite wing

Anytime the player in the middle catches the ball, she's dangerous. Your players should pass there whenever possible. When the ball goes to one of the short corners, 4 has several options:

- set a screen for the player with the ball
- set a screen for the player in the opposite short corner
- cut to the basket for a pass, if she has an open lane
- call for the ball, if she's wide open

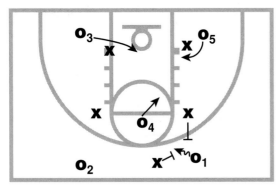

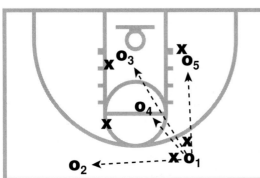

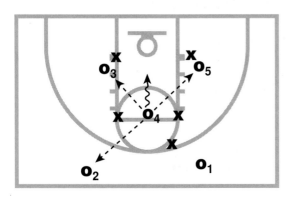

Ask the Coach

Question: "Two-Guard Offense" is a boring name. Can I call it something else?

Answer: The names I use in the book are just to call things something. Coaches call plays and formations all kinds of names, including colors ("Let's run Blue"), people's names ("OK, now we're going to learn the Abe Lincoln play"), animals ("We need to work harder when we run Tiger"), and schools ("We're going to call this the Carolina play"). Kids love colorful names, so let your imagination go.

One of the most effective passes in the Two-Guard Offense is the diagonal pass, either from an outside player to a short corner player, or vice versa. This pass is often available, particularly when playing against the 1-3-1 zone.

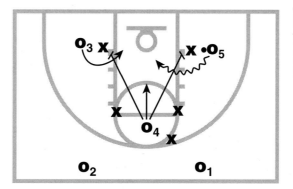

Ball in short corner in the Two-Guard Offense (left). Diagonal passes in the Two-Guard Offense (below).

One-Guard Offense

Use the One-Guard Offense when your team plays against zones with two-guard fronts (2-3 and 2-1-2 zones).

In this offense, 1 positions herself between two defenders at the top. Players 2 and 3 are at the wings. They're not on the same line with the two top defenders, but closer to the baseline so they split the gaps between the top defenders and the bottom defenders. Again, your best post passer should be above the free throw line. The other post starts on one side of the lane in the block area.

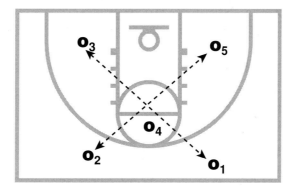

The offense begins when 1 dribbles to a spot in between the two top defenders. When they close in to stop her, she passes to an open wing or to 4.

When 1 passes to 2, player 5 posts up, 4 tries to get open in the ball-side elbow area, and 3 finds an open space on the help side for the skip pass. After 1 passes to 2, she relocates back to the top of the circle to be ready for a ball reversal pass from 2. At this point, 2 has several options:

- shoot, if she's open and in her range (she shouldn't shoot on the first pass)

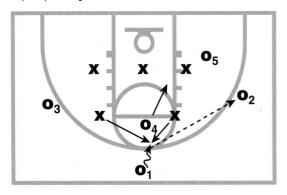

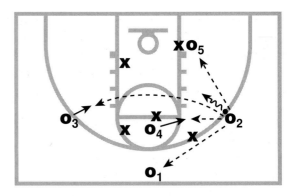

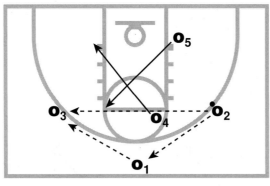

Initial movement in the One-Guard Offense (top left).
Wing options in the One-Guard Offense (top right).
Ball reversal in the One-Guard Offense (right).

- drive, if she has an opening
- pass to 5 posting up
- pass to 4
- make a skip pass to 3
- pass back to 1

When the ball reverses, either through 1 or 4, or from a skip pass, 5 cuts diagonally to the opposite elbow, and 4 cuts diagonally to the opposite block. Player 3 has these options:

- shoot, if she's open and in her range
- drive, if there's an opening
- pass to 4 posting up
- pass to 5 at the elbow
- make a skip pass to 2
- pass back to 1

Every time the ball swings to the other side, 4 and 5 cut diagonally. Whoever is on the block cuts to the opposite elbow, and whoever is at the elbow cuts to the opposite block.

The One-Guard Offense, like all good offenses, will eventually yield good shots, as long as the offensive team is patient.

Fast-Break Offense

A fast-break offense (also called *transition* offense) occurs when your players push the ball up the court as fast as they can after gaining possession of it. The goal is to take a good shot before the other team has all their players back on defense. Fast breaks can be run after a steal, a defensive rebound, a made free throw, or a made field goal. Fast-break offense is played at maximum speed with minimal structure. A team that's unprepared to defend against the fast break will find itself quickly outscored and out of breath. Fans like to watch fast-break basketball, players like to play it, and if your team is good at it, you'll like it, too.

A successful fast break results in a *numbers advantage*—a situation in which the offensive players outnumber the defenders. This can be a 1-on-0 situation (one player dribbling to the basket with no defender in her way), a 2-on-1, a 3-on-2, a 4-on-3, or a 5-on-4 situation. When the fast break involves only a few players from each team (a 1-on-0, 2-on-1, or 3-on-2 situation), that's called a *primary break*. When more players are back but the offense still has a numbers advantage, that's called a *secondary break*. Secondary breaks are for advanced teams, so I haven't included them in this book.

The first thing to teach your players is how to *run the lanes*. There are three imaginary *fast-break lanes*, each a third of the court (divided lengthwise). Each player runs up the court in a specific lane, based on the position she plays. There's a left lane, a middle lane, and a right lane, as viewed from the team's own basket.

Following are the principles of running a fast break:

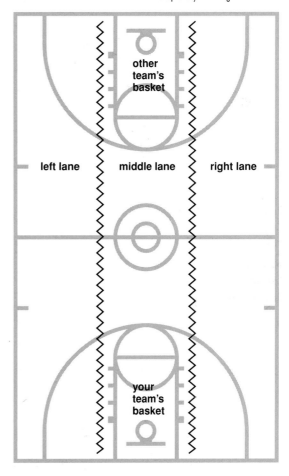

Fast-break lanes.

1. **Sprint up the court.** Much of the success of being able to score on a fast break is simply outrunning the defenders.

2. **Run the lanes.** How to run lanes is explained below.

3. **Get a shot off before the defense gets back.** If your players have a numbers advantage, they shouldn't wait for the numbers to even out. Even if the shot misses, your team will have a good chance for an offensive rebound.

4. **If someone is open ahead of you, pass her the ball.** The ball moves faster through the air than when someone dribbles it.

5. **If you can't pass ahead, dribble to the top of the circle.** This gives the dribbler more options than if she dribbles along one side of the court.

Who Does What on the Fast Break?

Everyone has a specific job on the fast break. Let's assume player 5 gets a defensive rebound. As she chins the ball and pivots away from her defender, 1 gets open on the same side of the court in the area of the free throw line

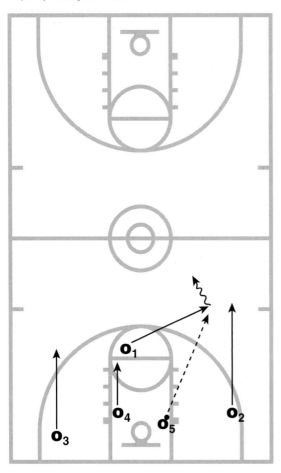

The fast break begins.

extended. She stands with her back to the sideline so she can see the court and yells "Outlet!" The break begins when 5 passes to 1.

As this happens, 4 runs up the court in the middle lane, 2 runs the right lane, and 3 runs the left lane. This is called *filling the lanes*. Players 2 and 3 run to the free throw line extended and cut in at a 45-degree angle to the basket. Player 4 runs down the middle of the lane and cuts to the ball-side block.

When 1 has the ball, she looks up the court to see if either 2 or 3 is open ahead of her. If not, she speed dribbles to the top of the circle. If a defender comes out to stop her, 1 comes to a jump stop and passes to 2 or 3 cutting to the basket. She then goes to the elbow on that side of the court.

If 4 beats her defender down the court, she'll be open for a pass and a layup. If a defender guards her, she posts up. After throwing the outlet pass, 5 sprints down the middle lane as the *trailer* (the last player on the fast break). She goes to the elbow opposite where 1 is and stops, ready for a pass.

At this point, if the fast break doesn't produce a good shot and the defense has three or

Ask the Coach

Question: No matter what I say, I can't get my girls to yell "Outlet!" They just giggle and look embarrassed. What am I missing?

Answer: Girls don't like to yell as much as boys do. They have to learn that it's fine to yell. At the next practice, line your players up and tell them to shout "Outlet!" as loud as they can, one by one. Tell them that the team will run a Victory Sprint (Drill 5) every time someone doesn't shout at the top of her lungs. Even the quietest girls will be yelling loudly in no time.

Question: My players insist on dribbling the ball up the court on the fast break instead of passing it. We miss out on some good shots. How can I change this habit?

Answer: In your next practice, have a little demonstration. Line up five passers in a line from one end of the court to the other. The first player is behind the baseline with a ball and the last player in line is on the block at the far basket. Have a player who insists on dribbling the ball up the court line up behind the baseline with a ball, next to the other player with the ball. At your signal, the passers pass the ball up the court and the dribbler speed dribbles up the court. It will be obvious which method advances the ball faster.

The fast break continues.

more players back, the ball should go back to 1, and a half-court offense should be run.

Teach the fast-break offense in stages. Begin with a limited number of players and work up to more players. See Fast-Break Drills in Part Two, Drills 60–65.

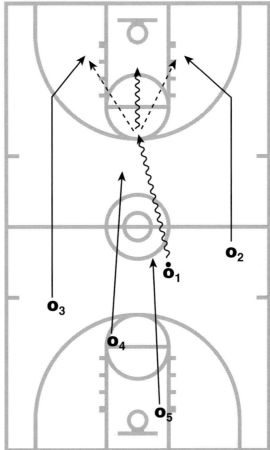

Out-of-Bounds Plays

In every game, there are times when the referee stops play, and your team has to inbound the ball:

- when a player from the other team commits a nonshooting foul
- when a player from the other team commits a moving violation
- when a player from the other team is the last player to touch the ball before it goes out-of-bounds
- when the alternating arrow awards a held ball to your team

The referee hands the ball to one of your players at the point where the ball went out-of-bounds or at the spot closest to the foul or violation. Your team then runs an *out-of-bounds play*, which is designed to inbound the ball successfully and provide your team with a good shot opportunity. The two kinds of out-of-bounds plays are sideline plays and baseline out-of-bounds plays.

Sideline Plays

If the ball is inbounded along either sideline, your team runs a sideline play. For all your inbounds plays, designate an inbounder. In the following plays, I assume that 3 is the inbounder, because most 3's are good passers and taller than the other perimeter players. The most important quality of your inbounder is that she's a smart passer under pressure.

Sideline Stack Play In the Sideline Stack Play, the other four players form a *stack* (a line) with the first player 6 feet from the inbounder. The players face the inbounder and stand together so no defender can squeeze in between them. The first player in line is player 1, followed by 2, 4, and 5. When they're ready, 3 slaps the ball to begin the play.

After the slap, 2 spins away from 3, uses 4 and 5 as screens, and sprints toward the basket. If the other team is playing tight man-to-man defense, this often results in a layup. Player 3 should always look for 2.

The second option is to pass to 1. As 2 makes her move, 1 takes four steps toward her team's basket and sprints by 3, looking for the pass. As she passes the inbounder, 5 sets a screen for her. If 1's defender is delayed by the screen, 1 has a chance for a drive to the basket or a 2-on-1 play with 2.

The third option is to pass to 4. While 1 and 2 are making their cuts, 4 turns away from 3, uses 5 as a screen, and heads away from the inbounder. This draws her defender with her, leaving the scoring area open for 1 and 2. If 3 passes to 4, 4 looks to pass to 2 or 1.

In the Sideline Stack Play, 5's role is to set screens. However, she's also the last option. After she screens for 2, then 4, she steps toward 3 and screens

First option in the Sideline Stack Play (left). Second option in the Sideline Stack Play (right).

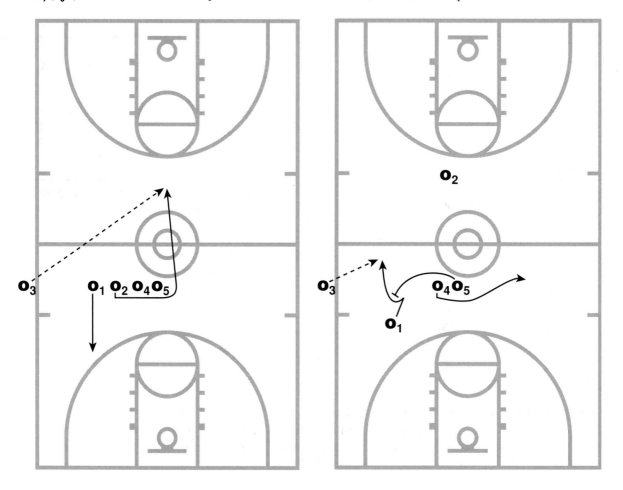

for 1. If 3 can't pass to anyone else, she passes to 5, who waits for 1 to come back and take the ball.

Remind your inbounders that if they can't make a good pass, they should call a time-out before 5 seconds have passed. It's better to use a time-out than give the ball to the other team. Of course, if your team has no more time-outs left, remind your inbounders that they can't call a time-out. A turnover is far better than a technical foul.

Baseline Out-of-Bounds Plays

When the ball goes out-of-bounds along the baseline behind the other team's basket, your team will run a baseline out-of-bounds play. These are excellent opportunities to get a good shot, because the ball is entered so close to the basket.

As with your Sideline Stack Play, designate an inbounder. Again, choose someone who passes well and won't panic. I again assume 3 is the inbounder (if your 3 isn't a good passer, choose someone else).

When the ball goes out-of-bounds, the referee gives it to the inbounder on one side of the basket. The inbounder should be 3 feet from the line, at the extension of the lane line. She shouldn't stand behind the basket, because the bottom part of the backboard restricts how high she can throw the pass. As with the Sideline Stack Play, the inbounder signals the start of the play by slapping the ball.

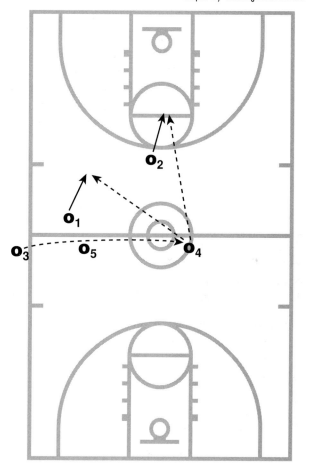

Third option in the Sideline Stack Play.

You should have one baseline out-of-bounds play for when the other team plays man-to-man defense and a second play for when the team plays zone defense. Teams that play zone in this situation usually use a 2-3 zone because the other zones don't have enough players near the basket.

I've included two plays for each defense: one that uses a box formation, and one that uses a stack formation. I've labeled them for the defenses for which they're suited. Change the names of any of these plays to make them recognizable to your players.

Against Man-to Man Defense Against man-to-man defense, run the Box Man Play or the Stack Man Play. In the Box Man Play, the other four players set up in a box formation. Player 1 is at the ball-side elbow, 2 is at the help-side elbow, 4 is at the ball-side block, and 5 is at the help-side block.

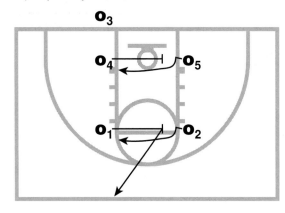

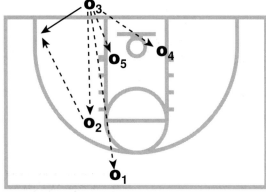

Initial movement in the Box Man Play (top). Options in the Box Man Play (bottom).

First ball slap in the Stack Man Play (left). Second ball slap in the Stack Man Play (right).

On the ball slap, 1 sets a cross screen for 2, and 4 sets a cross screen for 5. The first option is to pass to 5 for a layup. If 5 is taller than her defender, this can result in an easy pass and a jump shot from close range. The second option is to pass to 2, who either shoots an open jump shot, passes to 5 posting up, or passes to 3, who comes in from out-of-bounds to the ball-side corner.

After 4 sets her screen, she tries to post up in the lane. If she doesn't get the ball right away, she goes to the block that 5 vacated to avoid a 3-second lane violation.

After 1 sets her screen, she goes to the top of the circle to be the safety and the last option. If 3 can't pass to anyone else, she shouldn't panic, because 1 will be there. If 1's defender is guarding her closely, 3 should pass the ball over 1's head so 1 can race and grab it before her defender can. This is not an over-and-back violation. As long as the ball is entered from out-of-bounds, the rules allow a player to retrieve the ball in the backcourt.

The Stack Man Play starts out looking like the Box Man Play but has two ball slaps. At the first one, the four other players line up in a stack formation. Player 4 is first in line at the block, followed by 5, 2, and 1.

At the second ball slap, 1 drops back as a safety and last-resort pass, 2 cuts to the ball-side corner, 4 cuts to the opposite block, and 5 posts up where she is. Player 5 is the first option, because the area will be clear of everyone except for her and her defender.

The second option is to pass to 4. If 4 can post up in the lane, she'll be open for an easy shot. The third option is to pass to 2, and the last option

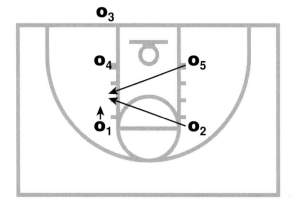

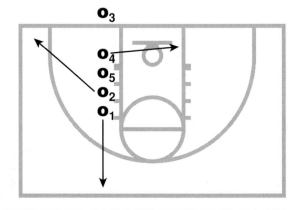

is to pass to 1. If this happens, 3 steps in to screen 5's defender, and 1 passes to 2 for a jump shot.

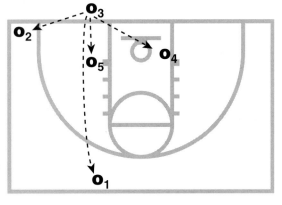

Against Zone Defense

Against zone defense, run the Box Zone Play or the Stack Zone Play. In the Box Zone Play, the players start in the box formation. At the ball slap, 4 screens the middle defender (usually the tallest player), 5 uses the screen to get open for a short jump shot, 1 sets a screen on the nearest zone defender, and 2 uses 1's screen to cut to the wing for an open jump shot. If 3 passes to 1, player 2 drops back to be the safety. If 3 doesn't pass to 1, player 1 goes to be the safety.

The first option is to pass to 5. Again, if 5 is tall, she'll often be open. The second option is to pass to 4, if 4 can post up. Players 4 and 5 must remember to leave the lane if they don't receive the ball to avoid the 3-second lane violation. The third option is to pass to 1.

The Stack Zone Play is another two-slap play. After the first ball slap, the players form a stack. At the second slap, 5 posts up on the farthest baseline defender, usually positioned inside the opposite block. If 5 is good at posting up, she'll be open for a layup. At the same time, 4 posts up on the block in front of the inbounder, 2 goes to the ball-side corner, and 1 goes to the 3-point arc halfway between the corner and the top of the circle.

The inbounder should first look for 5, then for 4. If they aren't open, she passes to 1. As the ball is in the air, 2 sets a screen on the closest baseline defender, who is usually

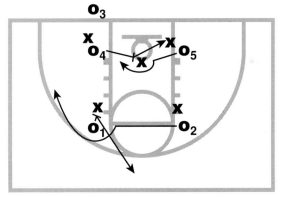

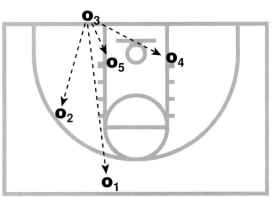

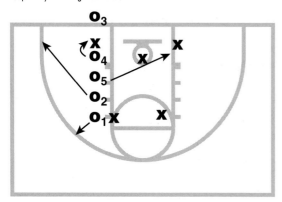

in the block area guarding 4. After 3 passes to 1, she goes to the corner that 2 vacated. With 2's screen, 3 will have an open jump shot almost every time.

After passing to 3, player 1 stays back as the safety.

Press Break

When a team guards the offensive players in the backcourt, the team is *pressing* them. The formations used to do this are called *presses*. Presses can be either man-to-man or zone.

Second ball slap in the Stack Zone Play (above). Options in the Stack Zone Play (right).

If you coach in a league that doesn't allow pressing, skip this section. Some middle school leagues allow pressing, but only for a limited time, such as in the last 2 minutes of the game. If the rules of your league allow pressing at all, you'll need to practice *breaking the press*, which means advancing the ball from the backcourt to the frontcourt under pressure.

Most pressing teams press after they score. It takes a second or two for a player from the team that was scored on to take the ball out of the basket and set up behind the baseline, which gives the defenders time to set up the press. Even when playing a team that doesn't start out pressing, expect them to press when the game is close, especially when time is running out and your team is ahead.

Teams that press want to:

1. **Cause turnovers.** They want to create confusion and bad decisions that lead to steals and easy scores.

2. **Speed up the offense.** Particularly against a team that doesn't play fast, the press forces them to play at an uncomfortable pace.

3. **Get the other team rattled.** When the press causes turnovers, the offensive players start to panic. This hurts the way they play at both ends of the court.

4. **Wear down the other team's ball handlers.** Most teams use their guards to advance the ball against the press. As the game goes on, the guards become tired. This makes them more likely to make mistakes.

For these reasons, you need to teach a *press break* (also called a *press offense*). These are the principles:

1. **Get the ball in the middle.** When the offense gets the ball in the middle, the press is broken. The V Press Break explained below has a player cutting to the middle for that purpose.

2. **Reverse the ball.** Attacking a full-court defense is no different than attacking a half-court defense. Ball reversal forces the defenders to change position rapidly. This presents opportunities for the offense to advance the ball.

3. **Look up the court.** Every time an offensive player catches the ball, she should first look up the court to see if someone's open.

4. **Pass before dribbling.** The ball moves faster through the air than on the floor. Your players should think of passing as the first option and dribbling as the second.

5. **Avoid traps.** Players who have the ball are likely to face traps. They shouldn't dribble into the obvious trapping areas.

6. **Try to score.** Don't settle only for advancing the ball up the court. Once the press is broken, run the fast break. If your team can score two or three easy baskets, the other team will likely *pull off* (stop) the press.

The V Press Break is suited to attack both man-to-man and zone presses.

As 3 takes the ball out of the basket, 1 and 2 set up at the free throw line, facing 3. Player 1 stands behind 2, her hands on 2's shoulders. Players 4 and 5 set up in the half-court corners, facing 3. They form the top of the V, and 1 and 2 form the bottom point.

On the ball slap, 1 pushes 2's shoulders to the left or to the right and cuts in the other direction on a diagonal line to the corner. Player 2 cuts to the corner indicated by 1's push. They shouldn't cut deep in the corner, or they'll put themselves in an ideal spot for a trap. To make it harder for the defenders to stay with them every time, 1 varies which way she goes. As 1 and 2 make their cuts, 4 cuts diagonally, sprinting hard toward the free throw line.

Player 3 waits to see who gets open. The first option is to pass to 4, because the press will

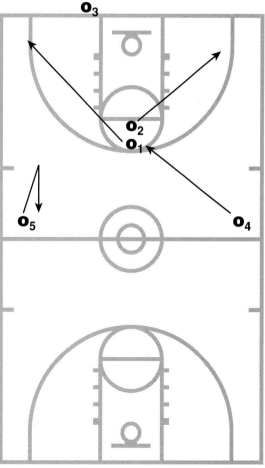

Initial movement in the V Press Break.

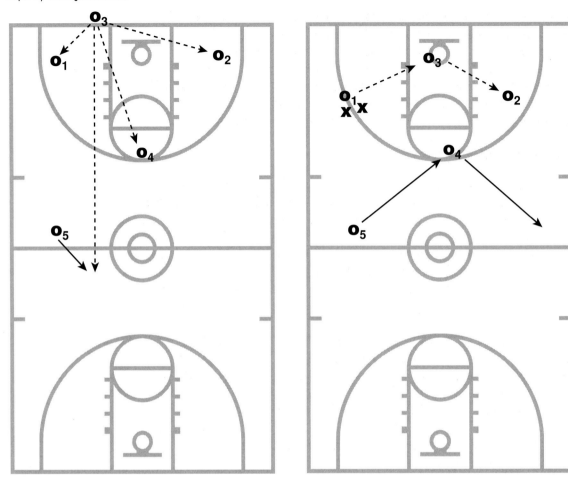

Options in the V Press Break (left). Ball reversal in the V Press Break (right).

be broken at that point. When 4 receives the pass, the other players sprint toward the other basket, looking for the fast break. If 4 isn't open, the second option is to pass to the player cutting toward the ball-side corner. The third option is to pass to the player heading toward the other corner. If 5's defender is more than a few steps in front of 5 and if 3 has a good arm, 3 can make a baseball pass over 5's head. It should be easy for 5 to outrace her defender and shoot a layup.

After 3 passes, she steps onto the court, staying near the basket in case 1 or 2 is in trouble. Player 3 is the means for ball reversal. If 1 can't dribble

Ask the Coach

Question: How do I get my kids to make good cuts in our press break? They cut like they're in slow motion.
Answer: Making cuts is another skill that needs to be learned and practiced. Most beginners won't have any idea what a cut is, much less how to make one properly. Teach your players to make cuts forcefully. They should sprint as they cut, then plant their foot and "explode" when they change direction.

or pass up the court, she passes back to 3, who immediately passes to 2. When this happens, 4 runs back to her original position, and 5 now runs to the middle. When 2 catches the ball, she first looks up the court for 4 or 5. If neither player is open and she's guarded, she passes back to 3, again reversing the ball. As long as the team crosses the midcourt line within 10 seconds, there's no limit to how many times the players can reverse the ball. Usually, after one or two ball reversals, the press is broken.

Last-Second Plays

Here's the situation. Your team is behind 22–21, there are only 5 seconds left in the game, and your team has to inbound the ball from under its basket. You call a time-out to talk strategy. After the girls run to the bench and sit down, you kneel in front of them. All eyes are on you. What are you going to say? You better have something to say besides "Let's go out there, girls, and play hard!" You better have your clipboard and marker ready to remind them how to run the last-second play you practiced just for this moment. Yes, it's time for 33X, the play that gets the ball to Molly on the baseline for her favorite shot.

You don't need to teach more than one last-second play. The same one can be used when you have to go the length of the court or when you inbound the ball near midcourt. Last-second plays can also be used when time is running out in the first half.

If you coach older girls, you may have a player who can throw a long full-court pass with accuracy. If so, put her as the inbounder. If you coach younger girls, you'll have no choice but to get the ball up the court with two or three passes. Here's a simple last-second play.

33X Play

Have your best passer be the inbounder. The other players set up in a box formation, two on the elbows and two at midcourt. Your best shooter should be at the nearest elbow, and your second-best passer in line with her at midcourt. At the ball slap, the two nearest players set screens for the far players, who come to the ball. After they screen, the screeners head toward the basket. The inbounder passes to the nearest player who is open. That player turns and passes to whoever is open up the court.

Ask the Coach

Question: I watched a game where 3 seconds were left, the defense was back at its end of the court, and the inbounder rolled the ball to a player who waited to pick it up. Why did she roll it? What was that about?

Answer: The clock doesn't begin until someone on the court touches the ball. If the defenders are back and time is running out, rolling the ball is a good tactic. Depending on how far up the court the ball rolls before an offensive player picks it up, this can save a couple of precious seconds.

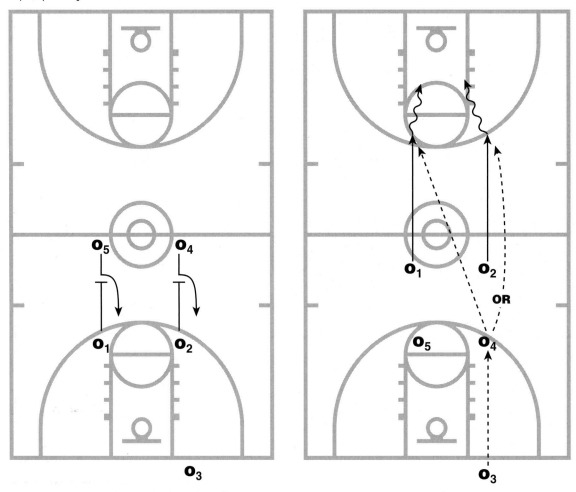

Opening Jump Ball

The game of basketball begins with a special play, the *jump ball* at the center circle. One player from each team stands inside the circle in the half nearest her team's basket. The players face each other. The other eight players line up outside the circle, wherever they want. When the referee is ready to start the game, he or she tosses the ball underhanded into the air between the two players, who jump and try to tip it to a teammate. The game is on.

Controlling the opening tip and scoring right away is a great way to start the game. Most teams use their tallest player for that purpose, on the assumption she's the best choice for a jump ball. Before you decide who will be your jump ball player, run a little test. Have your most likely candidates line up by a wall. Hand the first player a blackboard eraser with chalk dust on it. Tell her to take it in her strong hand and prepare to jump. On your signal, she jumps as high as she can and makes a mark on the wall with the eraser. The other players do the same. After they all jump, choose

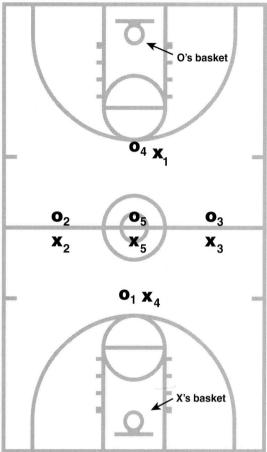

the player who made the highest mark. If there's a tie between two players, have them jump again.

After you've chosen your jump ball player, align the other four players. Unless your jump ball player is certain to control the tip, assume the other team will get the tip. Set up in a defensive alignment, where player 4 or 5 is back defending the basket, 2 and 3 are on the midcourt line, and 1 is on the other side of the circle. In games, 1 will be the primary target for the tip, but the jump ball player should learn how to tip it to other players if 1 is covered.

Practice the jump ball tip without defenders at first. When the jump ball player learns to tip it to any player whose name you call out, add defenders.

After the jump ball, the game is on (left)! Setup for a jump ball (right).

CHAPTER 4

Teaching Team Defense

Half-Court Defense

There are three kinds of half-court defense: man-to-man defense, zone defense, and combination defense (also called *junk defense*), which is part man-to-man and part zone. The latter defense has limited value, so I don't spend any time on it in this book.

Here are the principles of team defense:

1. **Stop the ball.** That's the first priority of any defense. Even if your man is left wide open, if you're the one defender who can stop a drive to the basket, leave your man and stop the ball.

2. **Keep the ball out of the lane.** This includes the high post area. It's better to let a team shoot from outside than have them shoot close to the basket.

3. **Make the ball go to one side of the court.** The defender guarding the point guard should force her to dribble to one side. This establishes a ball side and a help side. If the ball is in the middle, the offense has more options.

4. **Keep the ball on one side of the court.** Once the ball is on one side, try to keep it there. When the offense can reverse the ball, it distorts the defense and causes holes and seams. When the defenders keep the ball on one side, they have less to worry about.

5. **Drop to the basket.** The closer the ball comes to the baseline, the closer the defenders are to the basket. If the ball gets to the low post, five defenders should be nearby, trying to force the post to pass it back out. The farther from the basket the ball is, the less it can hurt the defense.

On pages 57–58, I talked about the importance of teaching man-to-man principles and techniques even if your team will play a zone. Before reading further, I suggest you reread that section.

Man-to-Man Versus Zone Defense

In deciding whether to play man-to-man or zone defense, consider the following:

- the experience and skill level of your players
- the competition your team is facing
- the relative strengths and weaknesses of each defense

Each type of defense has advantages over the other.

Man-to-man over zone defense:

- **More aggressive play.** Because the defenders guard a man as opposed to an area of the court, they play with more aggression and intensity.
- **More pressure on the ball.** In man-to-man, every dribble, every pass, and every shot can be contested. In a zone, the offense can pass the ball easily around the perimeter.
- **Better chances for turnovers.** This is a corollary of the first two points. Aggressive play and pressure on the ball mean more forced turnovers.
- **More fast-break opportunities.** Constant pressure on the ball and a faster pace give the defensive team more chances to run the fast break.
- **Better rebounding.** Because man-to-man defenders have specific players to guard, they know exactly whom to block out when a shot is taken. In a zone, defenders often are unsure which players they should block out.

Zone over man-to-man defense:

- **Easier to learn.** This is a major plus when you coach inexperienced play-

---

Ask the Coach

Question: My preference is to play man-to-man, but none of my girls have played it before. I'm concerned that we'll lose too many games while learning how to be good at it. If we play zone, we'll win at least a few games (few of the teams in our league have good shooters). What should I do?

Answer: Everyone who coaches younger players faces this question—do you opt for more wins or for preparing your players for high school basketball? Most good high school teams play man-to-man defense. If your players only learn how to play zone, the ones who go on to play in high school will be at a disadvantage. If you have quick, aggressive players, play man-to-man. The defense will take longer to teach, but once the players learn it, your defense will be tougher than if it were a zone.

On the other hand, if there's a big gap between the athleticism and experience of your players versus the competition, play zone. It's not worth suffering through 45–7 routs. Pack in the zone and force the other team to shoot from outside. Even if your team doesn't win any games, at least the scores won't be so one-sided.

Some coaches swear by man-to-man and some swear by zone. There's no right or wrong answer.

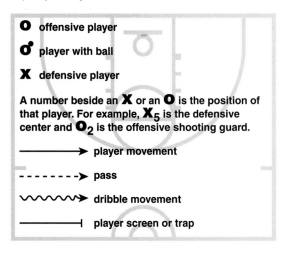

O offensive player

O⃗ player with ball

X defensive player

A number beside an **X** or an **O** is the position of that player. For example, **X₅** is the defensive center and **O₂** is the offensive shooting guard.

———————➤ player movement

- - - - - - - -➤ pass

∿∿∿∿∿➤ dribble movement

————————⊣ player screen or trap

Diagram key.

ers. It takes longer to learn how to play man-to-man than it does to learn how to play zone.

- **Easier to play.** Zone defenders have less square footage to defend. They have to worry about fewer offensive players. Zone offenses use screens far less than man-to-man offenses.

- **Better basket protection.** Dribble penetration is harder against the zone. Wherever a dribbler tries to drive, there's a defender ready to stop her.

- **Less chance of fouling.** Zone defenders are less likely to be out of position than man-to-man defenders. This means they are less likely to commit the reaching and blocking fouls.

- **Strong defense against poor shooting teams.** If a team doesn't shoot well from the outside, and the zone defenders can keep the ball out of the lane, the offense won't score much.

- **Not as tiring to play.** Playing man-to-man takes more effort than playing zone because the players have to cover more ground.

My teams play man-to-man defense, though every now and then we'll play a zone. The aggressive nature of man-to-man and its ability to force turnovers fits the style of basketball I like. After reading the rest of this section, you'll have a good idea of which defense suits your personality and your players.

Man-to-Man Defense

There are two kinds of man-to-man defense: sagging man-to-man and pressure man-to-man. In the sagging version, the defenders stay between their man and the basket. In the pressure version, the defenders stay between their man and the ball.

Sagging man-to-man defense is the more conservative of the two. It allows the offensive players more room to catch the ball, but the defender is in good on-ball position. The offense finds it easier to complete passes against this defense, but harder to drive to the basket.

Sagging man-to-man defense.

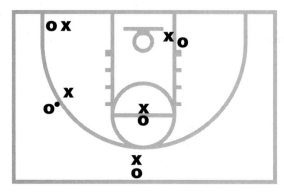

Pressure man-to-man defense uses the concepts described on pages 58–62 —on-ball defense, denial defense, and help-side defense. The four defenders guarding the players without the ball are either in the denial stance, with a hand

and foot in the passing lane, or in the help-side stance, with a hand pointing to the ball and a hand pointing to the man. The goal of pressure man-to-man defense is to contest every pass, dribble, and shot.

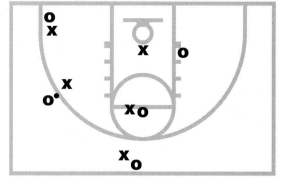

Here are the principles of pressure man-to-man defense:

1. When a pass is made, defenders should jump to the ball. They should get to their position before the ball gets to the receiver.

2. When the ball is above the free throw line extended and the defender's man is on the help side, the defender should keep one foot in the lane.

3. When the ball is below the free throw line extended and the defender's man is on the help side, the defender should be in the middle of the lane.

4. Defenders should know where the ball is at all times.

5. Defenders should know where their man is at all times.

6. Defenders should be ready to help. Players should realize that they can't help too early, but they can help too late.

7. Defenders should talk. Players should tell their teammates what they need to know.

Practicing Man-to-Man Defense

The best drills for teaching man-to-man defense are the *shell drills*, which can be done with anywhere from two to five defenders, but they are designed as a progression starting with two defenders. (See Drills 53–56 in Part Two.) The offensive players are set up in a particular alignment. They pass the ball, and the defenders adjust their positions and stances. The defenders aren't allowed to steal the ball—they must let the receivers catch it. The defenders' goal is to focus on being in the right position after each pass.

Practice one or more shell drills every practice. It will take some patience, but once your players learn these man-to-man principles, they'll be good defenders.

Other good drills that work on individual defensive skills and team defense are for your players to play 1-on-1, 2-on-2, and 3-on-3, without structured offense. An excellent drill that practices individual and team defense, along with offensive skills and decision making, is Three-on-Three-on-Three (Drill 65). This drill can be run in the half court or full court and is a good conditioning drill.

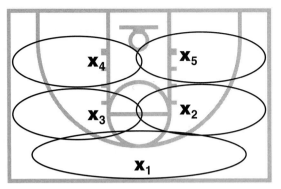

Areas of coverage in the
1-2-2 zone defense (above).

Areas of coverage in the
1-3-1 zone defense (right).

Zone Defense

In every zone defense, each defender has a specific area of responsibility. It's her job to guard any offensive player who enters her area, whether the player has the ball or not. In each zone defense there are areas that the defenders must cover.

1-2-2 Zone The 1-2-2 zone is a good zone to use when the other team shoots well. It covers the block areas well, as well as the high post area. Its major weakness is that it leaves a hole in the middle of the lane that can be exploited. Good offensive teams will send cutters into the middle of the 1-2-2 from the help side, so your players must be alert at all times and must talk to each other. When the ball is in the corner, the ball-side post defender must come out to guard the offensive player if she's a good shooter. This means the help-side post defender and help-side wing defender must change their position to protect the basket area.

The 1-2-2 offers trapping opportunities when the ball crosses the midcourt line. Have the top defender force the point guard to dribble to one side. As the point guard comes over the line, the two defenders trap her in the corner. After she picks up her dribble, the other three defenders look for chances to steal the pass.

1-3-1 Zone The 1-3-1 zone also covers the perimeter shooters well and has no hole in the middle. Its weakness is the coverage of the low post areas.

Areas of coverage in the 2-3
zone defense (left).

Areas of coverage in the
2-1-2 zone defense (right).

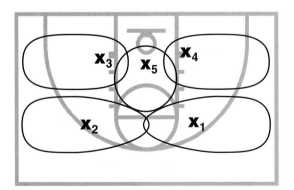

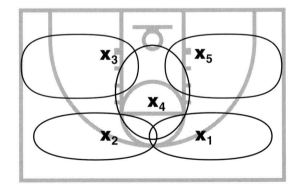

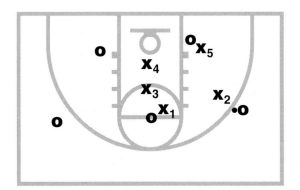

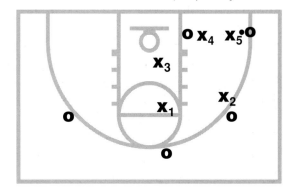

The back defender is responsible for a big area, so put a quick defender there (some teams put their point guard back there). Good offensive teams will try to exploit the low post weakness, so the middle defender and the ball-side wing defenders must be ready to drop down to help.

The 1-3-1 offers trapping opportunities in four corners. If you have quick defenders, they should look for chances to trap, particularly if the other team has shaky ball handlers.

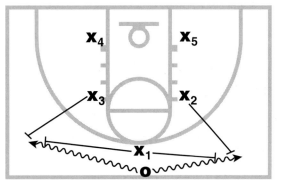

Ball on the wing in the 1-2-2 zone defense (top left). Ball in the corner in the 1-2-2 zone defense (top right). Trapping areas in the 1-2-2 zone defense (left).

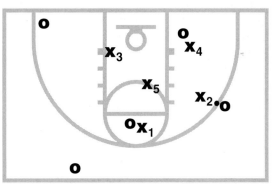

Ball on the wing in the 1-3-1 zone defense (left). Ball in the corner in the 1-3-1 zone defense (bottom left). Trapping areas in the 1-3-1 zone defense (bottom right).

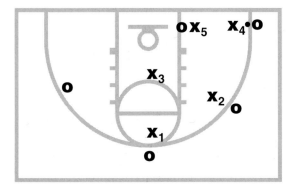

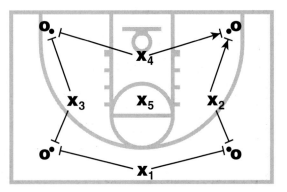

Ball on the wing in the 2-3 zone defense (right). Ball in the corner in the 2-3 zone defense (middle). Trapping areas in the 2-3 zone defense (bottom).

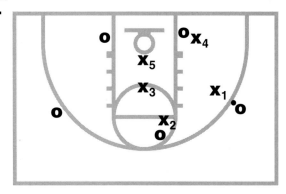

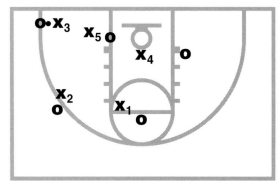

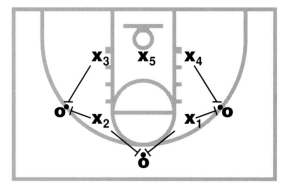

2-3 Zone The 2-3 zone is a popular zone defense. It provides excellent coverage around the basket and strong rebounding coverage. Its weakness is in defending the perimeter. When the ball is on the wing, the help-side top defender must guard the high post. When the ball is in the corner, the middle defender must drop to guard the low post if the ball-side post defender goes out to guard the shooter. The 2-3 gives up lots of out-side shots because two defenders cover a large area against three offensive play-ers. If the other team has good outside shooters, the 1-2-2 or 1-3-1 zone would be a better choice.

The 2-3 zone offers two trapping opportunities: one when the dribbler first brings the ball over the mid-court line, the other when the wing player receives the pass. For trapping to work in the second case, the ball-side posts must start out a few more steps away from the baseline. Otherwise, they won't have time to race out and set the trap.

2-1-2 Zone The 2-1-2 zone is a 2-3 zone with one difference—the middle player guards the high post area. However, when the ball drops toward the baseline, the middle player also drops down, as if she's in a 2-3. The 2-1-2 gives up some basket coverage but is strong in defending the high post. Other than that, everything about the 2-1-2 zone is the same as in the 2-3 zone, including the trapping areas.

Practicing Zone Defense

To practice zone defense, use the shell drills discussed on page 93 to practice man-to-man defense (see Drills 53–56). Start with just the players at the top

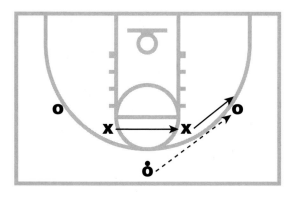 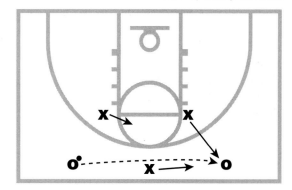

of the zone and place offensive players in the gaps. Have the offensive players pass the ball as the defenders change their positions as fast as they can. Work up to the point where the offensive players pass the ball after a count of one.

Then, add the rest of the offense and the other defenders. Make sure every offensive player receives and passes the ball. Have them reverse the ball through the point and the high post and by a skip pass. Have them pass the ball to the corner. Have the offensive players drive by a defender so the other defenders will learn to drop to the basket.

Top of 2-3 zone in the shell drill (left). Top of 1-2-2 zone in the shell drill (right).

Full-Court Defense

If your league allows pressing, even for 2 minutes at the end of the game, teach your team how to *press*, that is, how to defend the other team in the full court.

If you have aggressive, quick players, a full-court press is a powerful defense. A good pressing team dictates the pace of the game, scores easy points off steals, wears the other players down, and causes confusion.

Man-to-Man Press

If your team plays man-to-man half court, it makes sense to play man-to-man

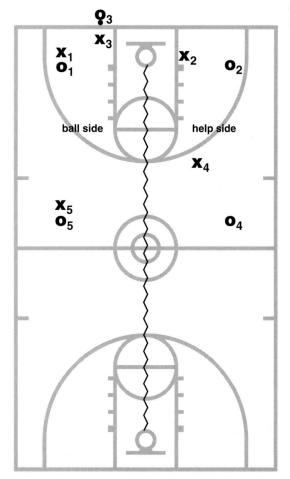

Man-to-man full-court press.

full court as well. After your team scores, as a player from the other team takes the ball out of the basket and prepares to inbound it, each defender runs to guard her man. The defender assumes the defensive stance and position based on the same man-to-man ball-side or help-side principles. If the player is one pass away from the ball, the defender guards her in the denial stance. If the defender is on the help side, the defender guards her in a help-side stance.

Zone Press

Full-court zone presses operate like half-court zones, where the defenders guard specific areas, not specific players. One of the simplest zone presses is the 2-1-2.

2-1-2 Press The defenders set up in a 2-1-2 formation with players 1 and 2 closest to the inbounder, 3 in the middle, and 4 and 5 on the back line. Players 1 and 2 try to deny the inbound pass but make sure the offensive players trying to get open don't get behind them. If the ball is passed in the middle, 1 and 2 trap the ball handler.

If the ball goes to an offensive player in the sideline area, the nearest defender forces the player to dribble along the sideline as 3 comes over to trap and the back defender guards against the forward pass.

Remind your players that the primary goal of the press is to cause the other team to work hard to bring the ball up the court. Even if the press doesn't result in a steal, the other team will start to wear down as the game goes along.

Trap in the middle in the 2-1-2 press.

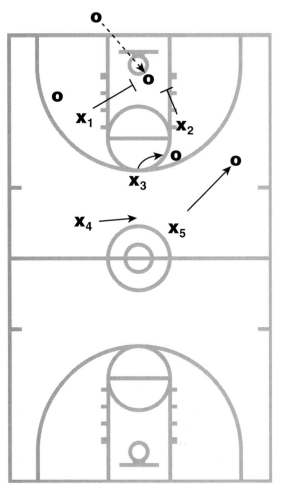

What to Do When the Press Is Broken

A press is broken when the ball goes to the middle of the court beyond the first wave of defenders. At that point, the defenders must stop pressing and must sprint toward their basket so the other team can't run a fast break. The defenders should head to the middle of the lane, looking over their shoulder every few steps to see where the ball is. Once they're sure there's no fast break, they can leave the lane to guard their respective man or zone.

Trap on the side in the 2-1-2 press.

If the other team has an excellent point guard who can break the press easily, the press can be a liability. Call it off, but consider double-teaming her in the backcourt after every made basket so the inbounder can't pass to her.

Defending Screens

Defending screens is one of the hardest things to do when playing defense. Your team likely won't encounter teams that screen much, but teach your players what do to if it happens. There are several approaches to defending screens, but most are too advanced for youth and middle school players. Teach the simplest approach—*switching on the screen*.

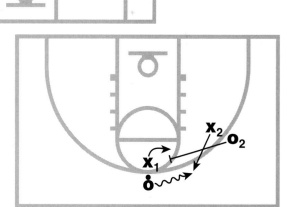

Switching on the screen.

Assume two defenders. Defender 1 guards the point guard at the top of the circle and defender 2 guards the player on the right wing. The point guard has the ball. Defender 2 sees that her man is running toward defender 1 to set a ball screen. She lets her teammate know by calling "Mary! Screen!" This alerts defender 1 that a *switch* is about to happen—the two defenders are about to trade offensive players. As the screener comes to a stop, defender 2 steps in front of the player with the ball to prevent a drive around the screen, while defender 1 turns her attention to the screener. Each defender now guards another player. The screen has failed to free up the player with the ball, and the switch is complete.

CHAPTER 5

The Season Is Underway... Now What?

Handling Your Players

In the Introduction, I mentioned the importance of being consistent in the way you handle players and not playing favorites. These points cannot be overemphasized. If you're not consistent, or if you show favoritism, you'll damage the team's trust and unity, which are so critical to having a successful season.

Chemistry 101. Coaches talk about having the right *team chemistry*. It's a vague term that means the players get along well and support each other through the good times and the bad times. It means that the players are team players, in that each player puts the team's interests above her own interests. When you have twelve to fifteen players on a team, each with her unique personality and goals, this is no easy feat.

Part of having a team with good chemistry is dumb luck—you're lucky to have players who are inclined to be team players—but most of it is based on the atmosphere you create as the team leader. I often tell my players, "It's amazing what can be accomplished when no one cares who gets the credit."

Team chemistry is like a strong wind. You can't see it, but you sure can see its results. If your team has good chemistry, it has a good chance of reaching its potential.

The team is number one. You've no doubt heard the saying "There's no 'I' in team." Coaches use corny clichés, but kids respond to them. Encourage and praise team play. At the University of North Carolina, Coach Dean Smith was the first coach to have his players acknowledge assists. After scoring, the player who scored pointed to the player who passed him the ball that led to the scoring opportunity. This habit has become commonplace across the country. Emphasize the unselfish things that are just as important to a team, like making assists, setting screens, diving on the floor for loose balls, and taking charges.

Everyone's role is important. A key part of having good chemistry is hav-

Ask the Coach

Question: I have four beginners who aren't skilled players. I'm having a hard time making them feel good about their contributions. Any suggestions?

Answer: Keeping every player on a team happy is a challenge. With only so many minutes of playing time available, the kids who play the least can become discouraged and lose confidence.

Part of how you avoid that is in choosing your team in tryouts. Sure, you want to have some stars. But every team needs kids who know they're not as skilled but are glad to be on the team. When you choose your team, pick a few players who you think will be happy in a limited role.

Another part of their satisfaction is how you treat those players in practice. If you cater to the best players and give them most of the attention, you'll lose the other players. However, if you go out of your way to make the less-skilled players feel as important to the team as the more-skilled players, they'll feel included. Again, what you do is more important than what you say.

ing players accept their roles. A successful team needs capable starters, capable middle-game players, and capable end-game players. It needs shooters, rebounders, defenders, and ball handlers. Your best players will have more than one role, but most of your players will have only one or two roles. Early on, identify what role each player will have and talk to her about her role.

Your challenge is to have each player accept her role. Each girl will do this only if she believes her role is important. Coach Smith also developed the "Blue Team" concept when he coached. The Blue Team consisted of five players who were not as skilled as the starters but who knew their roles and were proud of them. When Coach Smith put them in games to rest the starters, they gave several minutes of all-out effort. Their goal was to play great defense and protect the ball on offense. When they came out of the game, the home crowd always gave them a standing ovation. The Blue Team was an excellent example of players with limited skills accepting their limited roles.

Every year in preseason, I sit down with each player and talk about her role. I never give anyone more than three roles. More than three is too much to think about.

Motivating Your Players

I don't claim to have a fail-safe method to inspire a group of players to do their best in every practice and in every game. However, I've learned there are certain approaches that can help motivate your players.

Provide positive reinforcement. Most people respond to praise, and girls are no exception. When a player does something that deserves praise, let her know. Be specific. "Good job" is fine—coaches often say this—but "Good rebound" is better. When a player learns a new skill, praise her. However, don't overdo praise. If you give nonstop praise to your players, though you might mean it every time, the praise becomes less meaningful.

Avoid negative reinforcement. It's your job to point out mistakes so your players can learn. The trick is pointing things out the right way, not the wrong way.

First, be clear, matter-of-fact, and not angry. Saying "Remember to use your inside foot as your pivot foot" with a smile is a lot different than saying it with a glare or a frustrated sigh.

Second, never make criticism personal. Never say "Jennifer, what's wrong with you? Didn't you hear me?" or "Everyone else understands what we're doing. Why don't you?" Comments like that destroy a player's trust in you, not to mention the embarrassment you'll cause. It's much better to say "Let's review the play again" or "Try it again, this time cutting to the short corner right away."

Third, when you criticize, include a positive comment. Saying "I like how hard you work to get open, Melissa, but next time show a good target with your hands" tells the player you also appreciate what she has learned.

Fourth, don't criticize any player too much. If you criticize one player more than others, she'll feel singled out. What's the right amount of criticism? It varies from player to player, but if you see a player looking uncomfortable or embarrassed, you should stop. You'll have players who'll make the same mistake over and over and players who won't grasp simple concepts, but refrain from excessive criticism. There's no need to keep telling a player what she already knows—that she's doing it wrong. Dip into your bag of patience and smile.

Building Team Unity

A big part of good team chemistry is your players knowing and trusting each other. You can't dictate that everyone likes each other, nor can you force it, but you can do things that encourage closeness and trust. I tell my players, "You don't have to like each other, but you have to learn how to work with each other."

Team activities. Every now and then, get your team together for a social activity, like going out for pizza or bowling. If I think my players need a break from practice, I sometimes rent a good sports movie for us to watch together (*Hoosiers* is a classic). You could take your kids to an amusement park or for an overnight camping trip (along with a few other responsible adults, of course).

Team-Building Exercises

There are a number of team-building exercises you can do to help your players learn more about each other and trust each other more. Every year, my players go to a "ropes" course, where they face a difficult physical challenge together and learn how to communicate and work together.

The following ideas are suited to younger players.

Blindfolded Partners You'll need blindfolds for this exercise (pinnies work well). Split your team into pairs, pairing up girls who don't know each other well. Have one player in each pair blindfold her partner. Instruct the seeing players to guide their blindfolded teammate to a specific destination without leading or touching the teammate. They can only use words to guide the blindfolded players. Pick a safe destination away from flights of stairs or cluttered areas. Every pair has to finish before the exercise is over. What's the reward for the winning pair? Perhaps they can get out of running sprints that day. After every pair finishes, have the blindfolded players cover the eyes of their partners, and run the exercise again.

I Like You Do this exercise before practice, before the players' hands are sweaty. Print sheets of paper that say at the top: "I Like You Because . . ." Put each player's name on a sheet and put the sheets in a box. The players pull out a sheet, go to the sidelines where they can have some privacy, and write a reason why they like their teammate. The sheets go back in the box. At the next practice, give each player the sheet with her name on it so she can read what a teammate said about her. Do this exercise several times throughout the season so each player receives positive comments from more than one teammate.

Circle Drawing I do this exercise with my players every year, and they love it. It takes about an hour. In the locker room (or any open area, if you don't have a locker room), I give each player a sheet of poster board (2 feet by 3 feet). On the floor are crayons, markers, and colored pencils. I ask them to draw a big circle, which is a basketball. Then I explain, "Any way you want, divide the basketball into four parts. Draw only pictures—no words allowed. First, draw a picture of what you want to be doing five years from now. Next, draw your personal goals for this year—not just for basketball, but for school or whatever. Third, draw the team goals for this year. Last, draw your favorite toy when you were younger." The players spend a lot of time on this. Once they're finished, they display their drawings on an easel and explain them to their teammates. Then we tape each player's drawing to the back of her locker with two-sided tape. Our lockers are open, so every time the players walk into the locker room, they see their posters. (If you don't have lockers, players can take their drawing home and hang it their bed-room.) They enjoy this exercise, and everyone on the team learns a lot about the other players from it. I find that after we do this exercise, the players start forming relationships. The team starts developing chemistry.

Injuries

You don't need medical training to be a coach—that would eliminate 99 percent of all coaches—but you should know when a player is injured and when she's hurt. Injuries (sprained ankles, concussions, torn cartilage or

For any injury that is not a fracture (like strains and sprains), think RICE:

Rest the area to avoid further injury, but continue to move the injured area gently. Early gentle movement promotes healing.

Ice the area to reduce swelling. Apply ice to the affected area for 20 minutes and then leave it off for half an hour. *Note:* Don't use ice on a player who has circulatory problems.

Compress the area with an elastic wrap (when icing, secure the ice bag under the wrap). Compression reduces swelling and promotes healing. If a player has an ankle injury, leave her shoe on with the laces tied.

Elevate the injured area above the level of the heart. Elevation is especially effective when used in conjunction with compression. Continue to elevate intermittently until swelling is gone.

ligaments, pulled muscles, and broken bones) are serious matters. Hurts (temporary pains from bumps and bruises) are not. Given the physical nature of the game of basketball, bumps and bruises happen. Most players who are hurt can play with some pain, but some kids have a low pain threshold. Never make someone play if she doesn't want to.

Pay attention to injuries. The last thing you want is to allow an injured player to play and make the injury worse. If a player is injured, she shouldn't play again until her doctor and parents give their approval. You'll find that injured players want to rush back into playing before they're ready. Don't be swayed by their enthusiasm ("I'm fine, Coach! I really am!") or the need to get their scoring ability back on the court. Unless you write "M.D." after your name, don't try to be a doctor. The risks to the player's health are too great.

Ask the Coach

Question: I have a player who complains a lot in practice about not feeling well. She looks fine to me, but I let her sit out when she says she feels "bad." This never happens in games. She's always ready to go. My assistant and I are starting to wonder if she's faking it in practice. What should we do?

Answer: Anytime a player complains about not feeling well, take it seriously until proven wrong. Whenever a player says she feels "bad," mention it to the person who picks her up after practice. You may learn about a medical condition the player has that you should know about (parents sometimes leave out important information on the medical release). Maybe the parent isn't aware that his or her daughter feels sick. Maybe the player has something serious going on, like a virus that hasn't been checked out yet. Or, the player could be faking.

Some kids will do anything to get attention. If they don't get it positively because they're not doing what they're supposed to be doing, they'll get it by pretending to be hurt. Maybe they'll use "I don't feel well" as an excuse to get out of working hard. I had a player like that a few years ago. I could predict when she was going to be "injured" or "hurt" because she needed attention. After a big game, she wanted to sit out because she felt she deserved not to practice hard the next day. I finally called the player's bluff. I told her if she didn't practice that afternoon, it would hurt her preparation for the next game, and I couldn't start her. Magically, the problem went away.

When an injury happens to one of my players, after our trainer checks her, we move the player to the other end of the floor, away from the team bench. There's no need to have her situation distract and alarm the other players. Keep the rest of the team focused on what they're working on.

I have a rule that if a player doesn't practice the day before a game, she can't play in the game. Even if a player is sick, I want her to attend practice, because the next day she might feel fine and be ready to play. If a player is so sick that she can't attend practice, she's too sick to play the next day.

You'll have to be flexible about this rule with your players because they depend on other people to drive them to and from practice. A parent who has a hard time leaving work will be reluctant to bring his or her daughter to the gym just to have her sit and watch. Judge every illness and injury on a case-by-case basis. You don't want someone with a contagious illness hacking and sneezing on the sidelines, possibly infecting the rest of your team.

Dealing with Parents

Most parents will be positive about you and the team. Unfortunately, it only takes one or two unreasonable parents to taint what is otherwise a fun, productive season. You can't do anything to avoid unreasonable parents, but here are some things you can do to reduce the likelihood that parents will be upset:

Be accessible. Encourage parents to let you know when they have questions or concerns. Tell them you want to solve small problems before they become big problems. Give them your phone numbers and e-mail address in the handout.

Communicate. Parents don't like schedule surprises. If you forget to inform them that practice was canceled but they drove their daughter over in the snow anyway, expect some complaining phone calls.

Explain team rules and expectations up front. Be specific. If the consequence for missing practice is no playing time in the next game, tell them before it happens. The parents of a player who misses practice might still grumble, but they can't say you didn't warn them.

Get used to reality. Coaches can't please everyone. If a player is upset, it's likely that her parents will be upset, too. And if the parents are upset, you'll probably hear about it. Do your best to listen to unhappy parents, fix what you think needs fixing, and move on. Just like sneakers and layups, the occasional unhappy parent is part of coaching basketball.

Be calm under fire. When you find yourself face-to-face with an unhappy parent, take him or her aside so the conversation is private. It's no one else's business. Listen carefully to what the parent is saying. Wait until the parent finishes airing out all the grievances before responding.

If you're angry and emotional, tell the parent you need to think about it overnight. If you made a mistake, admit it and apologize. If your assistant or another player did something to upset the parent, you may have to talk to

Ask the Coach

Question: Should I let parents watch practice?

Answer: Some coaches do and some don't. I don't allow parents at my practices because I believe they distract their daughter. It's more complicated at the youth and middle school level. Parents are part of the landscape because they drop off and pick up their daughters. If a parent gets there 5 to 10 minutes early and watches the end of practice, I'd have no problem with that. However, if a parent starts to come and watch practices with regularity, I would have a problem with that. Somewhere between those examples, there's a line. You have to decide where to draw that line.

Question: A dad of one of my players is a former college player. During the games, he sits right behind our bench and yells instructions at his daughter. He has a booming voice, so everyone in the stands can hear him, as can his daughter, who looks at him when she runs up the court. She sometimes doesn't do what I want her to do, because it's not what he told her to do. This is becoming a big problem. What do I do?

Answer: Welcome to the "frustrated coach" syndrome, exhibited by the parent who was a player, or maybe is a coach, or who maybe is just an overeager fan. The frustrated coach thinks he knows a lot more about basketball than you do. This might be true, but what he doesn't realize is that shouting instructions to his daughter puts her in a difficult situation—do I listen to Dad, or do I listen to Coach? Talk to the dad before the next game. Tell him you appreciate his support and enthusiasm, but he can't coach his daughter during games because she already has a coach.

Question: A mom called me up last night, demanding to know what I have against her daughter. She said her daughter is very upset and thinking about quitting the team. She said the girl who started in front of her daughter played 22 minutes in the last game while her daughter played 6. She can't understand why that happened when her daughter is obviously a better shooter. I was caught unaware and didn't know what to say. I told her I'd call her back. What should I tell her?

Answer: Let her know you're doing your best to have her daughter improve her skills. Tell her that a big part of playing time is based on what goes on in practice and that it's impossible for someone who hasn't been at practice to make an informed judgment on how much anyone should play. Remind her that you don't discuss other players with parents. If you don't placate the mom, don't worry about it. You've done all you can.

Question: A dad of one of my players volunteered to run the clock at our games. He seems like a nice guy, but after hearing horror stories about hostile parents, I'm leery. Should I say yes to the guy?

Answer: While we coaches have to deal with an unhappy parent now and then, they are very much in the minority. Most parents are nice, reasonable folks. By all means, say yes.

the individual involved. Depending on the circumstances, you may need to be a peacemaker. Above all, be calm and professional, even if the parent isn't. If the parent becomes heated, tell him or her you'll be glad to continue the conversation when he or she calms down. Just because you're the coach doesn't mean a parent has the right to speak to you rudely or abusively. If you and the parent can't resolve the matter, take it to a higher authority like the athletic director of your school or the head of your league.

Set boundaries. The prime issue that makes parents unhappy is playing time. Most parents aren't objective about their daughter's skills, nor are they basketball experts. They think their daughter is a better player than she is. Some coaches have a policy of not discussing playing time with parents. Some will talk about playing time. I tell parents that I'll talk to them about anything they want to talk about, except that I won't discuss how I coach the team, and I won't discuss other players. We have a player on our team whose dad coached her in high school. On his team, she was a star, but on our team, she's not. That's been difficult for him. I've reminded him that that he isn't at the practices and doesn't see what we coaches see.

Over my career, I've had good relationships with parents. I've had only a few unpleasant situations. One season I had a father who came into my office and carried on about his daughter—playing time and other issues. He tried to intimidate me with a gruff, hostile manner. I told him calmly that he couldn't talk to me like that. I walked over to the door and opened it for him to leave. He stood and said, "Coach, you're right. I'm sorry. I was wrong." We talked for a few more minutes, and he left. He never spoke to me again about his daughter. He came to all our games and supported us and was never a problem again.

Playing time is the major issue on parents' minds, but it's not the only issue. The list of possible parental dissatisfactions with the coach includes playing the daughter in the "wrong" position ("Can't you see she's a shooting guard and not a point?"), not recognizing her obvious talents ("She's the best shooter on her summer league team"), ruining the daughter's shot ("She didn't used to miss like she does now"), and so on. You may be lucky and not have to handle an unhappy parent in your first season, but, sooner or later, you'll have your turn at it.

CHAPTER 6

Game Time

You've done your best to prepare the team. You've emphasized fundamentals. Your players have worked hard. Now it's time for the first test, a Saturday morning game against your first opponent.

Are the girls ready? Will they remember anything? Will they take good shots and not throw the ball all over the gym? How will they fare against another defense? Will they fall apart or rise to the occasion? You're about to find out. It's game time!

Mind-Set and Expectations

Naturally you're excited and even jittery. You've looked forward to this day for weeks. You've put a lot into it. But step back for a moment. Put yourself into the right mind-set.

Be cool and calm. Hide your jitters. If you act uptight, your players will see it, and that will make them uptight. They're anxious enough as it is. Don't make it worse. Joke around a bit. Loosen them up. Be positive. It's your job to be the calming influence.

Expect mistakes. Basketball is a game of continuous mistakes. Have you ever seen a game with no turnovers or no missed shots? I haven't, and don't expect I ever will. You'll see your players do boneheaded things, like dribble off their feet, pass to the second row in the stands, and heave up wild shots that have no chance of going in the basket. You'll see them confused about what to do on offense and where to be on defense. The best you can hope for is that your team makes fewer mistakes than the other team makes. The team with fewer mistakes will probably win the game. Just remember . . . no basketball team on earth plays mistake-free.

Expect ugly losses. Coaches at all levels experience games where the other team looks like the Los Angeles Lakers and their team looks like the Keystone Cops. This is part of coaching. If you coach long enough, you'll have your share of ugly losses. If you expect them, you'll be able to keep them in perspective when they happen.

Ignore the refs. This is easy advice to give but sometimes hard to follow. The referees have a very difficult job. In a one-sided game, no one pays much attention to the calls they make. However, in a hotly contested game, every call becomes a meaningful part of the action. Some fans think every call against their team is flat-out wrong. Extreme fans consider the calls part of a grand plot hatched by the refs to skew the game in the other team's favor. The reality is that there are good refs and not-so-good refs. Many youth and middle school refs are inexperienced (just like you!), which increases the chances they'll make mistakes. You'll likely see a lot of inconsistent refereeing and, now and then, some bad refereeing. Regardless, give the refs a lot of leeway. They're trying to do their best, just like you are. If you must protest a call, do so with great respect. While you won't change the call—protesting never does—your behavior will serve as a good example for your players.

Show good sportsmanship. Before the first game, talk to the team about sportsmanship. Define it. Give examples of good sportsmanship and bad sportsmanship. Make it clear that any display of the latter will result in taking a seat on the bench. Your actions will be more important than your words. No matter what the score is, no matter what you think about the other team, stick to the principles of good sportsmanship. Don't criticize their players or coaches. Shake their hands after the game and tell them they played a good game.

Win with grace. Teach your players that winning requires humility. Never laugh at the other team or gloat in victory. You may have scored more points, but their effort deserves respect.

Lose with grace. It's more fun to win than it is to lose. Nothing you tell your players will change that fact. Yes, a few teams go through a season undefeated, but 98 percent of all teams lose games, and many lose most of their games. Teach your players that losing is opportunity to improve. As long they learn, they'll get better. Stay positive during and after a tough loss. If your players see you react as if the loss is the end of civilization, they'll think that's how they should react. Life is full of disappointments. Learning how to lose with grace can be one of the most lasting skills you'll teach your players all season.

Pregame Routine

Many teams are unstructured in their pregame routines. The players seem to do what they feel like. They might shoot for a while or stretch for a while, and they chitchat about things that have nothing to do with basketball. When they warm up, they do so at half speed. Maybe this approach works for some teams, but I don't recommend it. Your pregame routine should be structured with two goals in mind: to warm up your players' bodies and to warm up your players' minds.

Huddling up before the game begins.

Many players think warming up means running around to get their hearts pumping. The physical preparation is only half of it. It's just as important to prepare mentally and emotionally for competition. We've all seen teams that come out *flat* at the start of the game. They don't have the intensity and energy of the other team. They seem dazed by the action, a step slow. The result? The other team out-hustles them for loose balls, out-rebounds them, and scores easy fast-break baskets. After 4 minutes, the flat team is down 13–2, and the pumped-up team has all the momentum. Even when the flat team finally wakes up, it has to play the rest of the game in catch-up mode. Nine times out of ten, even with a valiant comeback effort, the flat team can't make up the gap.

Game warm-up drills should include ball handling, shooting, defense, and rebounding. They should be designed so the players break into a sweat (note that no matter how hard some players work, they never sweat!). Choose drills that have worked well in practice. Warming up before a game is no time to introduce a new drill.

Throughout warm-ups, the players should be serious and focused. To pump themselves up before the opening jump ball, your team should gather at midcourt and do a brief ritual. Some teams lock arms, some teams hold their fists together, arms pointed to the ceiling, and some teams yell ("Intensity!"). It doesn't matter what your players do, as long as they're focused and together. Don't dictate what the ritual should be, even if you think it's silly or too "girly." It should be their ritual, not yours. If it's something they create, it will be more meaningful.

Ask the Coach

Question: I realize each team warms up in only one half of the court, but does it matter which half it is?
Answer: Before the game, each team warms up at the far basket, that is, the basket they will be shooting at during the first half. Before the second half, each team warms up at the near basket.

Choosing a Starting Five

The players who start the game are responsible for getting the team off to a good start.

As a general rule, choose your five best players for this role. An exception should be made if one of your best players isn't comfortable starting. Maybe she feels too much pressure and needs time to settle her nerves. This isn't a bad thing. One of the most important roles on any team is the first player who is substituted into the game, a player who provides instant energy on defense, offense, or both. Many successful teams consider that first off-the-bench player as their sixth starter.

Unfortunately, players and parents focus way too much on who starts and who doesn't. Beginning at the start of the season, deemphasize who starts. Explain that the team needs players who contribute in many ways —players who get the team off to a strong start, players who keep the momentum going until the end of the half, players who get the team off to a great start in the second half, and players who help the team finish strong. This goes back to the importance of having each player accept her role.

If your team or league has an equal-playing-time policy, this minimizes your decisions on who starts. In this case, make sure that every player starts at least once during the season. This will be more meaningful than you can imagine. The least-skilled player on the team will always remember the time she started a basketball game.

Substitutions

If you coach in a school or league that mandates equal playing time, you'll play everyone based on arithmetic—24 minutes of game time divided by twelve players means everyone plays about two quarters. Your only decisions are who should play in which quarters. There are two approaches. You can play your best players in quarters 1 and 3, hoping that in quarters 2 and 4 your other players can hang on. Or you can split the team into two balanced groups. The trade-off is you won't have a powerhouse group playing at any one time, but you also won't have a unit in the game that can lose

---

Ask the Coach

Question: I'm having trouble choosing my starting five. My team is full of beginners. No one stands out. How do I pick the starters?

Answer: Start by identifying your best team players. Then, from that group, decide who is best at the key skills. Don't get hung up on positions or size. Put your best ball handler at 1, your best shooter at 2, and your best rebounder at 5 (she may not be your biggest player). Pick the two best defenders and put them at 3 and 4.

ground quickly. My choice would be to have the balanced group, but a case can be made for either approach.

If you coach a team without stipulations on playing time, the decisions you make about substitutions will be significant. Developing a sense about when to substitute takes experience, but here are a few rules of thumb:

Take out tired players. When you see one of your kids gasping for air, bending over, holding the front of her shorts, give her a rest. Tell your players to let you know when they're tired. Some players don't do this because they want to stay in the game. Notice who's tired and take them out.

Take out players who aren't hustling. A player who doesn't sprint back on defense must be physically or mentally tired.

Put in players who don't play much. It's not right to keep your less-skilled players on the bench indefinitely. How are they going to learn if they don't play? Every player on your team should play in every game, even if your school or league doesn't require it. And not just for 37 seconds. That doesn't do anyone any good, least of all the player and her confidence.

Put in less-skilled players with better players. Don't put all your weakest players in at the same time. This doesn't give them much chance for success. Mix them in with a couple of your better players so they can be part of a good combination.

Put in new players when it's a blowout. If you find yourself behind or ahead by an insurmountable lead, put in everyone who hasn't played much. If the other team *clears its bench*—takes out its starters—clear your bench, too. If the other team leaves its best players in until the bitter end—inconsiderate coaches do this—use the player-mixing approach.

Substitution Procedure

Subs must follow a certain procedure when coming into the game. They check in at the scorers' table and kneel in front of it until the referee stops play and motions for them to come in. Each sub runs in, calling out the name of the player she's replacing. As they pass each other, the player coming out tells her replacement who she's guarding ("I've got 22"). This bit of communication is critical. Without it, the sub won't know where to be on defense.

To make sure my players talk to each other during the substitution procedure, I have the player who's coming in carry a towel and hand it to the player coming out. That way, the communication is more likely to happen.

Time-Outs

In high school games, each team is allowed five time-outs during regulation play: three 1-minute time-outs called *full time-outs* and two 30-second time-outs (and an additional time-out during each overtime period). Youth and middle school games are shorter, so there aren't as many time-outs. Before the first game begins, check with the referee so you know how many time-

Ask the Coach

Question: I have a player who double dribbles every time I put her in the game. I take her out right away. We work on dribbling every practice and she does fine, but in games she falls apart. What can I do besides grin and bear it?

Answer: You and the player are in a bad cycle. If you keep taking her out right away, her confidence will keep going down, which will mean she'll keep making mistakes. Change the dynamics. The next game, find a time when you can keep her in for at least 3 minutes, maybe at the end of the first half. Tell her before she goes in that you have confidence in her and that she's going to play for the rest of the half.

If some players make one mistake, they'll then make two or three more because they can't let go of the prior mistake. With these players, I'll take them out and tell them to settle down before I'll put them back in. Once they get back in, they're fine. Each player reacts differently to mistakes.

Question: In our last game, the referee came over and warned me about making "improper substitutions." He said if we kept doing it, it would be a technical foul. This was in the heat of battle so I'm not sure what he meant. What could it have been?

Answer: The rule is that before a player can be put in the game, she must check in at the scorers' table. On some courts, there's an X marked on the floor in front of the table for that purpose. The player must wait there until the referee blows the whistle and signals her in. Two things sometimes happen with young players. They're so excited to get into the game that they jump from their seat and run out on the court. Or they'll run out prematurely from the scorers' table. Both violations can result in a technical foul, though most referees will never call it. They usually will just warn you to keep your players from coming into the game too soon.

outs you can call. Most coaches try to not use up their allotment before the end of the game, in case they need to call a time-out during the critical last minutes.

Calling a time-out when you have none left is an automatic technical foul. One of the most famous instances of this was in the 1993 NCAA Men's National Championship game, when Chris Webber of Michigan called a time-out near the end of the game, which gave North Carolina free throws and the ball. Some people think this was the difference that allowed North Carolina to win the game. The lessons are clear: always know how many time-outs you have left and don't call one if you don't have one.

Good coaches don't waste time during time-outs.

When to call a time-out is a matter of instinct and strategy. I call one when I think my team is out of control or when I want to stop the other team's momentum. A time-out can change the flow of the game. Sometimes, when we have a lead and the other team is catching up, I'll call one to pause the action and regroup. I don't call time-outs to change the offense or defense because I can do that from the bench. Younger players aren't as able to change on the fly, so you might have to call a time-out if they're in an offense or defense that isn't working.

Here are some key points for managing time-outs:

1. Know how many time-outs you have before the game starts.

2. Give an assistant the job of keeping track of your team's time-outs, so at any time you can find out how many you have left.

3. Save one or two time-outs for the end of the game, if possible. If you use them up too early, you may regret it at crunch time.

4. Try not to call a time-out near the end of a quarter. If there are less than a couple of minutes remaining, hold off. Hopefully your team won't lose much more ground. However, if the other team is scoring points in quick succession, don't hesitate to call a time-out to regroup.

Time-Out Procedure

Since time-outs are very short, don't waste a second. Organization is the key. Practice having your players run on and off the court during time-outs, so they're ready to listen to you in no more than 10 seconds.

In a **full time-out** (1 minute), have your players run to the bench and sit down. The rest of the players should stand to make room for them. Someone should hand each seated player her water bottle, so the player doesn't have to wander along the bench looking for it. While the players are getting settled and drinking water (insist that they drink, even if they think they're not thirsty), take 10 seconds to confer with your assistants and plan what you're going to say.

In a **30-second time-out**, there isn't enough time for the players to sit. They should run to you and huddle on the court as you talk to them. The rest of the players should gather around so they can hear what you're saying. They should bring water bottles so the players in the game can have a drink.

Make sure the players not in the game are attentive during time-outs.

Ask the Coach

Question: I called a time-out the other day so we could change from zone to man-to-man defense. After we went back on the floor, half the girls stayed in their zones. I thought I was crystal clear. What can I do differently to get my point across?

Answer: All coaches experience moments when it seems that your players didn't hear a word you said. For many young players the game is a blur. Their minds are going a million miles a minute, and they have a hard time focusing and listening.

Don't assume a player understands what you're saying when she nods her head. Go overboard in making your point. Repeat the instruction, looking each player in the eye. Then ask, "So, what defense are we playing now?" Even if they answer, "2-3 zone," there's no guarantee they got it, but at least it's a good possibility. You'll find out in the next minute.

They might be going into the game at any moment and should know what the strategy is. When a time-out is called, have your bench players stand and clap as the players run off the floor. This lets the players know that their teammates acknowledge and appreciate their efforts.

In a time-out, be clear and brief. If you overload your players with too much information, the time-out will be wasted or, worse, you'll cause confusion. In a full time-out, give the players no more than two things to think about. In a 30-second time-out, give them only one.

Following are some good things to communicate during time-outs:

- **A change in strategy.** "Number 32 is killing us. Let's double-team her every time she gets the ball," or "We're changing to our 2-3 zone for the rest of the half."
- **A likely change in the opponent's strategy** (this often happens when the other coach calls the time-out). "They're probably going to press, so set up in our V break, OK?"
- **A change in intensity.** "They're beating us to all the loose balls. Let's start playing with more energy."
- **A change in tempo.** "We're playing too fast and making too many mistakes. Slow it down. Play at our pace, not theirs."

Time-outs are also useful for giving your team a rest. If your players look tired, but the other team's players don't, call a time-out to give them a much-needed break. Don't feel like you always have to say something meaningful. If they just need a rest, let them drink water and catch their breath.

Halftime

Give your players the first minute or two of halftime to talk among themselves, go to the bathroom, and drink water. During that time, talk to your assistants and plan what to say. When you talk to the players, be brief. If you're covering X's and O's, use the whiteboard. Visual aids help kids understand better. Tell them who will start in the second half. Remind them that the team that starts out strongest in the first 3 to 4 minutes of the second half often controls the rest of the game.

Whether you have your players shoot or run a drill before the second half starts is a matter of preference. Whoever played in the first half is obviously warmed up, but if you plan to put in players who haven't played yet, they should warm up. If your team shot poorly in the first half, you might want everyone to shoot. If your team is playing well, however, let the players do what they want, whether it's shoot, stretch, or rest on the bench.

With 30 seconds to go, call them over and huddle them up. Repeat the key instructions (remember, a maximum of three things), and send them out to play.

Pep Talks

Every coach has his or her repertoire of *pep talks*, little speeches designed to fire up the team. My view is that the coach can inspire the team only so much. True motivation comes from within.

Most of the time, my halftime comments have to do with X's and O's and execution of the game plan. Every now and then, if we're playing way below our capabilities, I'll let my players have it. That can mean different things to different coaches. It's OK to be honest, opinionated, and loud, but it's not OK to make personal attacks, use bad language, or be abusive.

One of the times when I let my team have it made it into the Women's Basketball Hall of Fame in Knoxville, Tennessee. In a room called the Locker Room, there's a big screen set up where you can choose to see halftime speeches made by different coaches. One of the choices is a speech I made to my players at halftime during a game against North Carolina State. We were playing absolutely awful basketball, so I made the players put their hands on their hearts to check if their hearts were beating. As it happened, the game turned around, and we won it. A Hall of Fame employee told me my speech is the most watched speech of all. I don't know whether to be proud or embarrassed.

Ask the Coach

Question: We played a terrible first half the other day. The starters made lazy passes and didn't move their feet on defense. At halftime, I thought about starting five different players in the second half, but I didn't because I didn't want to hurt their confidence. The starters played better in the second half, but the scoring gap was so big we lost by a lot. In hindsight, should I have started the other players?

Answer: Don't hesitate to change the lineup when a starter isn't playing the way she should, especially if she's not working hard, like not moving her feet on defense. Not starting sends a strong message. In the locker room, say something like "In the first half, we didn't hustle like we can, so I'm going to put in some other players to see what they can do."

Question: We played so lousy in the first half the other day that by the end of it I was hopping mad. At halftime we went into the locker room, and I ripped into the team. I've seen plenty of college coaches rip into their players on the bench, so I figured it was fine to let my emotions out. It's not like I hit anyone. Now that I've calmed down, I feel bad about getting on them like I did. Was it wrong to let them have it?

Answer: It depends. Don't model your behavior after what you see other coaches doing. Most coaches handle themselves well, but some coaches behave poorly when things don't go their way. They embarrass themselves and their players.

Always treat your players with respect and dignity. When times are toughest is when you should adhere to this principle the most. Your kids are counting on you to be an anchor, not a loose cannon.

There are certain actions that go beyond the realm of good coaching—profanity, screaming, throwing things, kicking things, putting your hands on a player, and berating a player. If you did any of the above, your behavior was unacceptable. Apologize to your players and the parents, and don't do it again. If you have a habit of repeatedly doing any of the above, get out of coaching. You might have good intentions, but you're not emotionally ready to handle the responsibility.

Statistics

Some coaches think statistics, or *stats*, have little value. Some coaches use stats as a major factor in their decision making.

I lean toward the second approach. In practice, my assistants chart information like shooting percentages so I can see how each player progresses as the season goes along. At halftime, I always check certain key stats before talking to the team. I look at *points in the paint* (baskets scored in the lane area) and *outside points* (baskets scored outside the lane area) for both teams. I want to know how each of our defensive strategies has done, how many times the other team has scored off our man-to-man defense, and so on. If the other team shot 2 for 16, we don't need to adjust our defense. If they shot 8 for 16, we need to change something.

Review the stats after each game. If you've never used stats before, this might seem like a waste of time. After all, you don't need a sheet of paper to tell you that their number 50 scored a ton of points. You're right— stats don't tell you anything new about the big picture. Their value is in pointing out less obvious things you didn't notice. It's learning, for example, that your shooting guard played a great game, though she scored only 2 points. She also had 5 assists, 4 rebounds, 3 steals, and didn't turn the ball over once.

Stats are useful in evaluating player progress. The numbers tell you which players are doing a better job on the boards than they were at the beginning of the season. When the season began, for example, your second-string 3 didn't contribute much, but now you see that she averages 5 points and 3 rebounds per game, while playing only 4 minutes each game. Imagine what she night do if she played 10 or 15 minutes a game. It's time to get her more playing time, isn't it?

The more you use stats, the more you'll come to appreciate them.

Stat Keepers

Assign an assistant or a parent to be a stat keeper during games. Don't assume the person knows how to do it, even if the person says he or she does. Keeping basketball stats correctly involves understanding several gray areas, such as turnovers and assists, which are subject to interpretation. Go over the stat sheet with the stat keeper. Have him or her keep stats for a scrimmage or two before the first game.

Keeping game stats isn't easy. Events happen so fast on the court even an experienced stat keeper can't keep up with everything. Assign another volunteer to be a spotter to help the stat keeper.

The stat sheet your stat keeper uses doesn't have to be fancy. A sample stat sheet is included in the Appendix (the sample sheet doesn't include shooting stats because those are kept by the person who keeps the scorebook).

Assistants

In addition to helping you run more effective practices, your assistants can help you do a better job of bench coaching.

Assign an assistant to keep track of fouls and time-outs for both teams. He or she should be able to tell you at any moment how many fouls each player on both teams has, how many team fouls each team has, and how many time-outs each team has left. You can't make good bench decisions without this information. If, after a nonshooting foul, the referee is about to hand the ball to your player for an inbounds play, your assistant should immediately tell you that it's the seventh team foul, and your player should go to the free throw line. Before you call a time-out in the closing minutes, the assistant should tell you what the time-out situation is so you can tell the players (remember—calling a time-out when you have none left is a technical foul).

Encourage your assistants to give you their opinions during the game. They might notice that a player is hurt or tired before you do. They might pick up that when the other coach yells "Blue," that means an isolation play for their shooter on the right side. They might suggest that your team try a different defense, since the other team has scored three times in a row against your 1-2-2 zone.

Assistants are there to help you and the team. It's foolish not to ask for and consider their opinions. Doing so also has another benefit—you'll make them feel more a part of the team. They'll realize that you value their contributions, and next year, when you ask, they'll be eager to help.

Creating the Best Game Plan

Before each game, create a *game plan*, a written list of strategies and tactics you'll use in the game. Here are some general guidelines:

Play to your individual strengths. If you have a good outside shooter, include a couple of plays to get her open for a shot. If you have

---

Ask the Coach

Question: The first game of the season is coming up. I don't know anything about the other team. I want to scout them. How should I go about it?

Answer: Unless you're in a highly competitive league with advanced players, *scouting* (watching a future opponent in person to see how they play) is overkill in youth and middle school basketball. That's not to say you shouldn't come early to watch the team you're playing next week. Casual scouting is fine. However, given that your players are still learning how to dribble and pass, taking the time to scout a team the way high schools and colleges do is over the top. Instead, use the first half of your games to scout. By halftime, you'll know everything about the other team that you need to know. If things aren't going well, make adjustments. That's what great coaching is all about!

a good 1-on-1 player, include a play that isolates her on one side of the basket.

Play to your team strengths. If you have a quick, aggressive team, go with man-to-man defense. If you have a tall team, pack in your defense so your rebounders are in good position to get the ball after a shot.

Neutralize the opponent's strengths. If the other team is good at running the fast break, designate two safeties whose assignment is to sprint back right away when the other team gets the ball.

Attack the opponent's weaknesses. If their guards aren't strong ball handlers, trap them. If their post players are smaller than your post players, pass the ball around the perimeter until there's an opening to pass it to the low post.

Part of your game plan is to decide:

- who the starters are
- who the first subs will be
- what defense you'll play
- what offense you'll play if they come out in man-to-man
- what offense you'll play if they come out in zone
- how you'll break the press, if it happens

Strategies and Tactics

There are no magic formulas when it comes to game strategies and tactics. It will take game experience and trial and error to learn what strategies and tactics might be best for each game situation. Notice I say *might*. There are plenty of other variables, including how well your players carry out the strategies and tactics you choose and what the other team does to counter them. Here are a few situations to consider:

When the game plan isn't working. This happens to every coach—a game when the other team is doing everything right and your team is doing everything wrong. As you watch, you wonder, at what point do I abandon the game plan?

Before scrapping the game plan, analyze the situation. Why are you behind? If your players aren't playing as well as they can—if they're sluggish, throwing bad passes, and committing silly fouls—this is a lack of intensity or focus, not a problem with the game plan. However, if your players are working hard but the other team has figured out how to get easy shots off your defense, it's time to think about trying another defense. Maybe something different will slow them down.

Game plans only go so far. There are times when no game plan works, times when, no matter what your game plan is, the other team is going to flat-out wallop you.

When your team is getting walloped. In this situation, *shorten the game,*

Ask the Coach

Question: Last week we were humiliated. The other team was excellent, which I had no trouble with. What angered me was that the other coach kept his starters in for the whole game, even though I put in all my subs. After the game I was tempted to say something to him, but I held my tongue. Should I have said anything?

Answer: Unfortunately, some coaches with dominating teams don't believe in good sportsmanship. They keep their best players in until the end, they continue pressing and fast-breaking, and they stay in man-to-man. This is a disservice to their players. When they're bashing a team of players who are nowhere near as skilled, they don't improve at all. Worse, they learn the wrong lesson about sportsmanship. My view is "What goes around comes around." Sooner or later, the coach you encountered will find his team at the bottom end of a mismatch and will get his own dose of humiliation. Maybe once he learns how it feels, he'll change his approach.

My teams sometimes play teams from "mid-major schools" (schools that don't play in one of the big national conferences). Though they're the underdog, the coaches of those teams are willing to play us at our gym because they know we won't run up the score. I've been in their shoes. I want their players to feel like they played a good game. It's simple—not running up the score is a basic part of good sportsmanship.

As for saying anything to the coach after the game, it would probably be a waste of words. That kind of coach would only get defensive or angry. However, I wouldn't hesitate to talk to the head of the league about it.

that is, reduce the number of possessions each team has. Would you rather have the other team have the ball sixty times or thirty times? Which alternative would likely result in a more lopsided game? Have your players slow the pace. Have them pass ball deliberately until they have a great shot. At halftime, deemphasize winning. Create different goals, such as "Let's hold them to 10 points this quarter" or "Let's score more points this half than we did in the first half." Make the goals challenging, but achievable. If goals are too easy, reaching them won't mean anything to your players.

When I first started coaching at the University of North Carolina, the women's program wasn't strong. We're much better now, but we had to crawl before we could walk, and walk before we could run. We crawled, we walked, we ran, and, finally, we're sprinting. But it took a very long time. If your team is struggling, be patient and persistent. Be realistic about the competition, be honest with your players, set doable goals, teach them fundamentals, and your players will have a successful season.

When your team is behind, but there's still a lot of time left. Don't panic. Make every possession count. Press. Try to cut the margin down a basket at a time. Teams that are way behind tend to panic and play faster than they should. They force passes that aren't there and take bad shots. If you're calm and focused, your players won't panic. If you act like the world is falling apart, you can count on it—things will fall apart on the court.

When your team is walloping the other team. When your team is outscoring the other team by a lot, don't *run up the score*—don't pile on the points unnecessarily. Show respect for the other team. Don't embarrass their players. Nothing will anger the opposing coach more than if it looks like you're trying to make a lopsided game worse.

If your team is ahead by more than 15 points at the end of the third quarter, it's obvious which team will win. Take out your first-string players, stop pressing, slow down the fast break, and switch to a zone defense. This is a good opportunity for your less-skilled players to get playing time and for your players to practice patient half-court offense. So what if the lead is down to 8 points by the end of the game?

When your team is ahead by 8 to 10 points. That's a nice lead, but don't let your players get too comfortable. Sometimes, teams that have a nice lead stop playing hard and lose intensity. When the other team scores a few baskets, their players start to believe they have a chance. They become inspired, and what was a 10-point margin is suddenly down to 4, with plenty of time left in the game. Emphasize to your players that they can't afford to relax, because when they do, the other team will sneak up on them. Don't run up the score, but keep the pressure on. Too many teams have learned the hard way that if they ease up too soon, they might find they're in a dogfight at the end.

Ask the Coach

Question: My team is winning by huge margins. In our last game, we stopped pressing after the first half, and I took out my starters in the middle of the third quarter. The other coach was still mad. What else can I do? I can't tell my players not to shoot, can I?

Answer: Some leagues have a *mercy rule*, a rule that says when the scoring margin exceeds X points, regardless of how much time is left, the game is over. Barring a mercy rule, you're faced with a legitimate question: how far should you go in calling off the dogs? You could go too far. For example, if you were to tell your players not to shoot anymore, and there were still 10 minutes left in the game, the other coach might not like that either. Most coaches don't want their opponent to stop trying. It's as if you're saying "Coach, your team is so rotten, my players can play bad basketball and still beat you." You have to find a balance between running up the score and telling your players not to not shoot anymore. Here are some ideas:

- Tell your players that only certain players (choose less-skilled players) can score. This makes them work to get the ball to the designated players and forces those players to get open.

- Tell your players that you want them to take only low post shots. This makes the perimeter players work on passing to the post.

- Tell your players that you want six passes or three ball reversals before a shot. This makes your players work on passing, moving without the ball, and making good decisions.

All these tactics will slow down the rate of your team's scoring, while your players practice things you want them to work on, and the other team won't feel like your team is giving them anything for free.

You might find that even after making these adjustments, some of the coaches are still mad. At that point, you've done as much as you can reasonably do, so shake their hand and forget about it.

Ask the Coach

Question: If we're ahead, but not by much, and they're scoring easily on our defense, would it be wise to switch to a 1-3-1 zone? We haven't practiced it, but I think it would throw the other team off balance.

Answer: It's unwise to play a defense or offense you haven't practiced. The players may nod their heads during the time-out, and you might think what you've diagrammed is as clear as water, but the odds are high that the players will go out on the floor confused. All it takes is for one player not to understand the unfamiliar concept, and the chance of success falls apart. You'll be more likely to slow down the other team if you try something you've practiced.

When your team is playing against a big scorer. Coaches look at this situation in one of two ways. Some say, "Number 22 is going to score a lot no matter what we do, so our goal is to keep the other players from scoring. There's no way she can score enough points to beat us single-handed." If you choose this approach, put your best defender on her and don't worry when she scores. As long as one of their other players doesn't score much, your team will have a good chance to win.

Other coaches say, "The key to stopping their team is stopping number 22. No one else can hurt us. If we can keep her to under 10 points, we should win the game." If you adhere to this approach, keep a fresh defender

Ask the Coach

Question: I'm confused about fouling at the end of the game. The rules say that an intentional foul results in two free throws. Yet I've seen games where the defender is obviously trying to foul the player with the ball, but the referee calls it a regular personal foul. Why isn't that an intentional foul?

Answer: This is a part of the game where referees, coaches, and players have an unspoken understanding. It's obvious to everyone watching that the defender is trying to foul to stop the clock. In that sense, fouls at the end of the game are intentional. However, the unspoken understanding is that unless the foul is excessive, like a two-handed push in the back, referees won't call it intentional. This is why you should teach your players how to foul intentionally without committing an intentional foul. The defender should go for the ball aggressively and try to steal it. If she can't steal it, she should make contact with the offensive player, so it's a foul. Fouling intentionally is a skill that needs to be learned and practiced.

Question: I heard a coach talk about his team making too many "silly fouls." What are those?

Answer: When coaches talk about silly fouls, they're talking about fouls players make that don't make any sense, such as:

- **A foul 60 feet from the basket.** Why foul someone that far away? They're not about to sink a shot from there.

- **A foul on a 3-point shot.** Unless your team is trying to stop the clock, this foul is a gift to the other team. Why give someone three shots from 15 feet when they're likely to miss one shot from 21 feet?

- **A lazy foul.** This is when the defender swipes at the dribbler, instead of moving her feet and getting in the proper on-ball defensive position.

on her. Try to wear her down. Tell your defenders to double-team her when she touches the ball.

When your team is in foul trouble. Remind your players to play smart defense: they shouldn't reach or swat at the ball, and they should move their feet and not their hands, and so on. If your team is in man-to-man defense, switch to zone. Players will be less likely to be out of position. Emphasize the importance of getting defensive rebounds. Offensive rebounders are often fouled.

Postgame Routine

After the game ends, meet with your players for a few minutes. Keep your comments to a minimum because the players will be distracted. If they won, they'll be too excited to listen. If they lost, they'll be too upset to listen. Be brief so everyone can go home.

If your players won, congratulate them on a job well done. Don't talk about any one player. Your focus should always be on the team, not on individuals. If they lost, try not to make them more disappointed than they already are. Don't talk about what they did wrong. Save that for the next practice. Remind them that they played their best, and that's all any coach can expect.

When I'm upset about how my team played, I try not to say much about it until the next day. After watching the tape, I might feel differently compared to how I felt during the game. If I were to let my emotions out right after the game, I might say something I'd later regret.

Learning from Games

Every game, win or lose, offers important lessons. A game is wasted if your team doesn't learn from it.

After the game, while your recollections are fresh, write down your observations. Use a blank notepad or fill out a game sheet (see the sample game sheet in the Appendix). Make notes about the other team (its tendencies on offense and defense, its best players, its strengths and weaknesses) and about your team (what worked well, what didn't).

This has two useful purposes. One, it serves as an excellent reference should you play the team again. Two, it serves as a basis for deciding what your team needs to work on as you prepare for the next game. Adjust your daily practice plans (see the sample in the Appendix) as needed.

Don't throw out your notes at the end of the season. You might need them in the future. You might be such a good coach that the powers-that-be will insist on you doing it again next year!

The Season Is Over . . . Now What?

Right after the season ends, have a team party. It should be casual, informal, and inexpensive. You can never go wrong with pizza as the entrée. Before

Looks like a happy team. Great job, Coach!

the party, decide what awards you want to give. You can buy inexpensive plaques and trophies at some sporting goods outlets.

This is the time to recognize outstanding performance and attitude. Be choosy about how many awards you give. If you go beyond three or four awards (for example, Most Valuable Player, Most Improved Player, Defensive Player of the Year, and a Spirit Award) you start to decrease the significance of those awards. Life doesn't hand out awards to everyone for outstanding performance, and neither should you.

After you hand out the awards, call up every other player and present her with a certificate of appreciation for playing on the team. Say something positive about each player.

Give a little speech. Tell your players how much you enjoyed coaching them and how much they improved. Tell them to work on their game between now and next season so they don't forget what they learned.

Thank your assistants for their contributions. Thank the parents for their support. Single out the team parent and any other parents who volunteered during the season. Eat a slice of pizza and enjoy the last time you'll be with the team. You'll realize that you're going to miss them. You've become attached to this great group of girls. That's one of the joys of coaching.

Before too much time passes, sit down and make notes on the season. Ask your assistants for their input. What could you coaches have done better? What drills worked, and what drills didn't? Which offenses and defenses should you use next year, and which ones should you scrap? What are you going to do off-season to improve your coaching? Is there a good clinic coming up in your area? Good coaches never stop working to improve.

When you look back on the season, you realize that coaching girls' basketball has enriched your life. It's a challenge and a lot of work, but it's also a joy. Be careful. If you coach again next year, you just might be hooked!

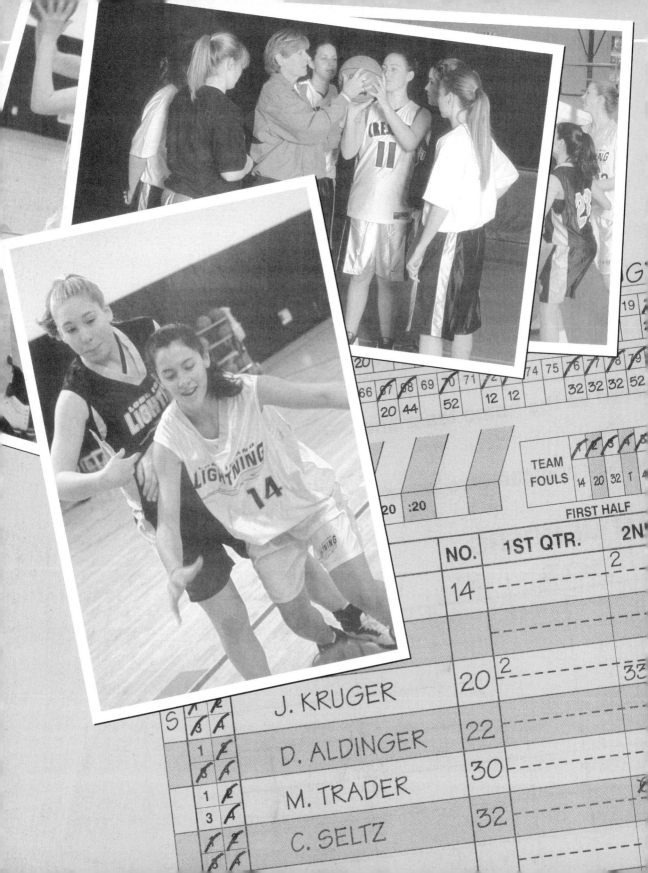

PART TWO

Drills: The Foundation for Development and Success

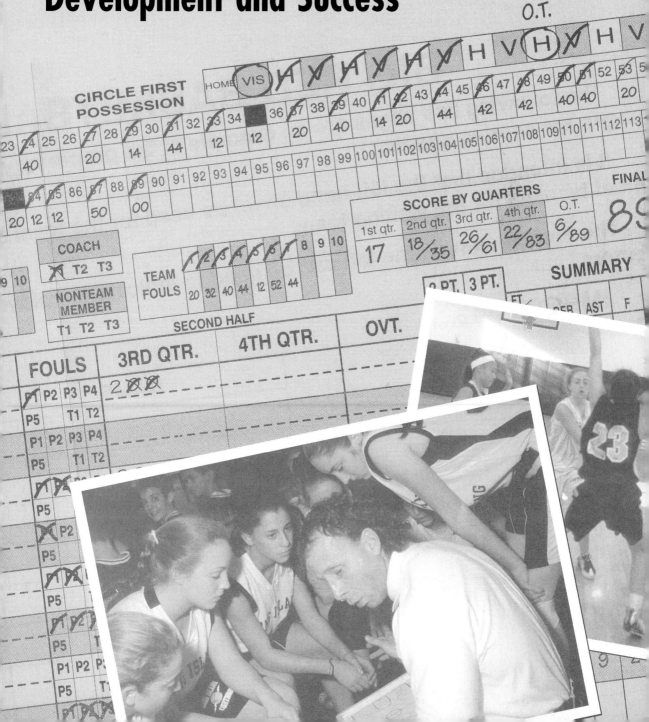

Footwork Drills

1. Pivoting and Jump Stop ☞

The players start on the baseline, each with a ball. Spread them out so there's at least 3 feet between each player. If you have a big team and need more room, have the players stand along one of the sidelines.

On your signal, the players dribble up the court slowly with their right hands. When you blow the whistle, they come to a two-foot jump stop, the ball on their hips, in the triple threat position. On your signal, they resume dribbling. Every time they hear the whistle, they come to a jump stop. When they reach the other baseline, they come to a jump stop and make a 180-degree forward pivot using their right foot as the pivot foot. They dribble back down the court, this time with their left hand, stopping and starting when they hear the whistle. As they get good at this, have them dribble faster.

After they dribble up and back twice, tell them to switch their pivot foot.

Variation: Have the players pivot every time they stop, protecting the ball from an imaginary defender. On your signal, they continue in the same direction. You can also have them pivot 180 degrees each time they stop and then continue in the new direction.

Emphasis: Encourage players not to lift or drag their pivot foot. Have them rip the ball across their body in a wide range of directions, from high to low and from side to side.

2. Protect the Ball ☞

Set up pairs of players, each pair with one ball. One player is the offensive player; the other is the defender. The player with the ball pivots while the defender moves around her, trying to pressure her. After 30 seconds, the players change roles and go again.

Emphasis: Players should move the ball in a wide range of motion, not a limited arc. Remind them to keep their elbows out.

3. Machine Gun ☞

Set up three lines across the court, facing you. The players are in a defensive stance. When you say "Go," they begin to *stutter step*, moving their feet up and down rapid-fire, lifting them only a few inches off the floor. When you point to one side, they swing step to face that direction for a moment, then swing step back to their original position. Younger players won't be able to last more than 15 to 20 seconds before stopping. Allow players to rest for 10 seconds and then go again. This drill is good for conditioning, agility, and improving foot speed.

Variation: After a swing step, the players remain doing the machine gun facing the new direction.

Conditioning Drills

4. Five in Seventy-Five

Set up a line of players along the baseline. Have a stopwatch ready or use the second hand on your watch. At your signal, the players sprint as fast as they can to the opposite baseline and back five times. Time how long it takes the last player to finish. Most high school players do this in less than 65 seconds, so you'll have to adjust for the age and fitness of your players.

Variation: Have players dribble a ball as they run, making jump stops and pivots at each baseline. Adjust the time to a reasonable standard.

5. Victory Sprints

Some coaches call these *ladders*. Line up your players along one baseline. They sprint up and down the court in this sequence: from the baseline to the near free throw line extended, back to the baseline, up to the midcourt line, back to the baseline, up to the far free throw line extended, back to the baseline, up to the far baseline, and back to the original baseline. This drill is good for conditioning and agility.

Variation: Have players touch the floor every time they plant their foot to reverse direction.

6. Victory Dribbles

The players follow the same sequence as in Victory Sprints, but they dribble a ball as they run. It's interesting to see that the players who run the sprints the fastest aren't always the players who dribble the fastest.

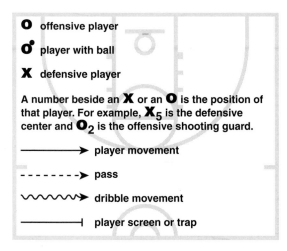

O	offensive player
O⃗	player with ball
X	defensive player

A number beside an **X** or an **O** is the position of that player. For example, X_5 is the defensive center and O_2 is the offensive shooting guard.

———————▶ player movement

- - - - - - ▶ pass

〰〰〰▶ dribble movement

————————| player screen or trap

	beginner
	intermediate
	advanced

Diagram key (left).

Degree of difficulty key (right).

Stationary Dribbling Drills

Set up your players in a ring around the center circle, each holding a ball and with several feet between each player. Choose a player or a coach to lead the series. Have the person lead the team through the following drills:

7. Ball Slaps 👉

Each player holds the ball in her right hand and slaps it with her left for 10 seconds. She then holds the ball in her left hand and slaps it with her right for 10 seconds. This warms up the hands.

8. Pound Dribble 👉

Each player dribbles with her right hand in a control dribble stance. The ball should bounce no higher than her knee and should hit the floor in hard bursts. After 30 seconds, the player switches the ball to her left hand and does the Pound Dribble for another 30 seconds.

Emphasis: Players should keep their head up and watch the leader in the middle. They should keep their back straight and not hunch over.

9. Ball Wraps 👉

Each player wraps the ball around her knees, her waist, and her head in one continuous motion. She then wraps the ball down to her knees, where she started. After 15 seconds, the players wrap the ball in the other direction for 15 seconds.

10. Crossover Dribble 👉

Each player practices doing a crossover dribble, keeping her hands below her knees and switching the ball from one hand to the other for 30 seconds.

Emphasis: Players should look up and get into a rhythm, swaying slightly from side to side.

11. V Dribble 👉

Each player dribbles with her right hand, dribbling the ball from side to side in front of her. The ball should make a small V as it bounces. After 30 seconds, the player switches to her left hand.

Variation: Have players dribble in a random pattern of crossovers and Vs. For example, they can do a crossover, then a V, then another crossover. Or, they can do a crossover, five Vs, then another crossover.

12. Ball Step-Throughs 👉

This drill is an advanced version of Ball Wraps (Drill 9). Each player does four leg wraps as follows: She wraps the ball behind her knees (wrap 1). When the ball is back to her original hand, she steps with her right foot, passes the ball between her legs, and wraps it around her front leg (wrap 2). When the ball is back to her original hand, she brings her right foot back and wraps the ball around both legs again (wrap 3). When the ball returns to her original hand, she steps with her left foot, passes the ball between her legs, and wraps it around her left leg (wrap 4). She repeats the sequence.

After 30 seconds, have the players wrap the ball in the opposite direction. Once the players get good at this, they'll be able to do dozens of wraps in a minute.

13. Figure-Eight Dribble

Each player spreads her feet wide and dribbles a ball between her legs in a figure-eight pattern. After 30 seconds, she dribbles in the opposite direction.

Variation: Have players dribble for 30 seconds around their right leg, using only their right hand. Then have them dribble around their left leg, using only their left hand.

Emphasis: Players should keep their head up as they dribble.

Other Dribbling Drills

14. Cone Dribble

Set up cones in a line from one basket to the next, with 6 to 8 feet between each cone. The team lines up under one basket, each player with a ball. On your signal, the first player dribbles with her right hand to the first cone. When she gets to it, she crosses the ball to her left hand and dribbles around the cone and to the next cone. When she comes to the cone, she crosses the ball to her right hand and dribbles around it. Each time she arrives at a cone, she crosses the ball to her other hand. After dribbling by the last cone, the player speed dribbles back down the court and gets in the line again.

When the first dribbler reaches the first cone, the second dribbler begins. The third dribbler begins when the second dribbler reaches the first cone, and so on.

Variation: Shorten the distances between the cones. This forces the dribblers to make more crossovers. Stagger the cones so they're in a zigzag pattern. This forces the players to maker sharper crossovers.

Emphasis: Players should keep the ball low when crossing over.

15. Dribble Tag

Kids love this drill. Everyone has a ball to dribble. Designate two players who are "It" and put them in the center circle. The other players have 5 seconds to go anywhere in the gym, other than in the stands (don't let them dribble where they can get hurt). When you say "Go," everyone starts dribbling, and the two players who are "It" go after the other players, trying to tag them with their hand. When someone is tagged or loses the ball, and thus stops dribbling, they're out. They go to the center circle and stand there dribbling until all the players are out. Pick two new players to be "It" and run the drill again.

Your players will quickly learn that they need to double-team the better dribblers in order to tag these players. As the season progresses, make sure every player has a chance to be "It."

16. Relay Dribble

Kids love this drill, too. Set up two lines of players behind the baseline. The first player in each line has a ball. At the signal, each player speed dribbles to the far basket, makes a layup, rebounds her shot, dribbles back down the court, makes a layup at the near basket, rebounds her shot, and hands the ball to the next player in her line. The drill continues until every player in each line has finished. When a player misses a layup, she shoots at the basket until she makes a shot. This is a fun drill that works on speed dribbling and making layups under pressure.

17. Full-Court Dribbling

Line up the players along the baseline, each with a ball. When you yell "Go!" players speed dribble with their right hand to the other baseline, come to a jump stop, and speed dribble back with their right hand. Then they speed dribble up to the other baseline and back using their left hand. Next they speed dribble up and back using alternating hands. Lastly they speed dribble up and back three more times, starting with their right hand, but every time you say "Cross!" they pause and then do a crossover dribble.

Variation: This is a good warm-up drill when players do it at three-quarter speed.

Emphasis: Encourage players to push the ball ahead of them and to get to the other end in as few dribbles as possible.

18. Zigzag Dribbling

Divide the players into pairs, each pair with a ball. The pairs form a line along the baseline, with the first pair at one corner. Each pair has an offensive player and a defender. The offensive player's goal is to dribble the length of the court in a zigzag pattern as fast as she can. The defender's goal is to turn the dribbler—force her to change directions with a crossover dribble. The defender uses a step-slide motion and at first doesn't poke at the ball. Once your players learn to protect the ball, the defender should try to poke the ball away (with her palm up to avoid fouling).

The drill starts with the first player dribbling with her left hand to the near elbow. After three dribbles, she crosses the ball to her right hand and dribbles three times to the midcourt corner. There, she crosses back to her left and heads to the near elbow at the far basket. When she crosses over again, she heads for the corner. The players sprint to the other end of the baseline and switch roles. The dribbler becomes the defender, and the defender becomes the dribbler. They run the same drill down the other half of the court, making the same zigzag pattern.

Run the drill for 3 minutes or until your players are tired. This drill is good for improving conditioning, the ability to handle the ball under pressure, and on-ball defense.

Emphasis: The dribbler should keep her body between the defender and the ball and should keep her head and nondribbling arm up.

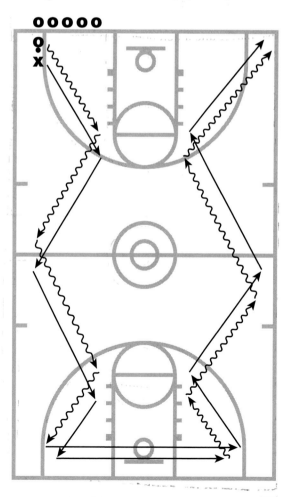

Zigzag Dribbling.

Passing Drills

19. Pairs Passing

Set up pairs of players around the court, each with a ball. The partners stand 12 feet apart and begin with two-handed chest passes. They pass for 30 seconds and then switch to one-handed push passes with their right hands. After another 30 seconds, they make left-handed push passes, then bounce passes, outlet passes, baseball passes, and curl passes.

Emphasis: Each player should give her partner a target. She should make a two-foot jump stop as she catches the ball and should keep her passes sharp and accurate.

20. Monkey in the Middle

This is the same game we all played in elementary school. Set up a line of three players with a passer at each end and a "monkey" in the middle. The distance between the passers is 12 feet. The passer must hold the ball until the monkey comes over to guard her. The passer works on ball fakes, pivoting, and ripping the ball for 3 seconds before passing. Change the monkey after 30 seconds.

21. Full-Court Passing

Set up six players as passers in stationary positions: four at the free throw lines extended and two at the center circle. The rest of the team is in a line near the basket. Each of the first four players in line has a ball. The idea is for the players in line to go up one side of the court and back down the other by passing, not dribbling. The only time the ball hits the floor is before shooting a layup. As the first player passes and receives passes, she keeps running up the court. When she reaches the far basket, she shoots a layup, gets the rebound, and starts back the other way. As soon as the first player reaches midcourt, the second player passes to the right-side sideline player, and so on.

22. Machine Gun Passing

Line up six passers in a half-circle, each with a ball. A middle passer is positioned at the center of the half-circle, 6 to 8 feet from each perimeter passer. The drill starts with a passer on one end passing to the middle player, who passes back.

Full-Court Passing.

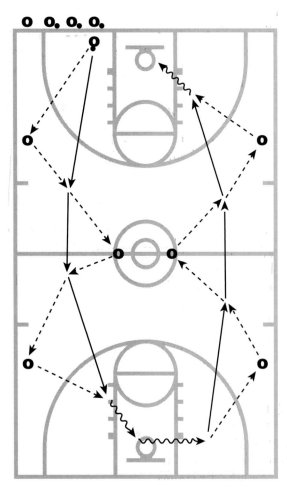

The second player then passes to the middle player, who passes back, and so on. The goal is for the passers to make rapid-fire, hard passes. Continue the rapid passes for 30 seconds and then replace the middle player. This drill is good for hand-eye coordination.

23. Triangle and Trap

This drill practices passing out of a trap. Set up three players in a triangle, 12 feet apart from each other, one with a ball. Have two trappers in the middle of the triangle. The trappers trap the player with the ball, who can't dribble and can't pass until she's trapped. The passer works on passing around the trap and splitting the trap. After she passes, the trappers trap the new player with the ball. Run this drill for 1 minute and then rotate the players so everyone can practice this important skill.

24. Three-Man Weave

Set up three lines of players on the baseline — one under the basket, the other two at the short corners. The first player in the middle line has a ball. The object is to pass the ball up the court as quickly as possible. At the signal, the player with the ball passes to the player on the right and cuts behind her. The player with the ball passes to the player on the left and cuts behind her. The third player passes to the first player and cuts behind her. As they head up the court, they make a weave pattern.

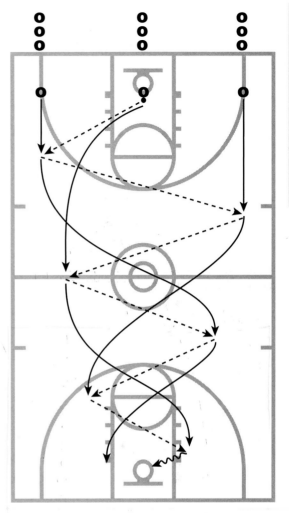

Three-Man Weave.

When the ball is passed to a player near the basket, she shoots a layup. The closer of the two other players takes the ball out of the basket and starts the weave back the other way. When one of the players makes a layup at the original baseline, the next player in the middle line catches the ball as it drops through the basket, and three new players start up the court. The goal is for the ball to never hit the floor, other than one dribble before the layup.

25. Four-Line Passing

This drill works on protecting the ball, passing under pressure, ball fakes, curl passes, and on-ball defense. Four players stand in a line with 10 feet between them. The two middle players are defenders. A player at one end has a ball, and the drill begins when the player nearest her comes up to guard her. The player with the ball must pivot for 3 seconds (she counts

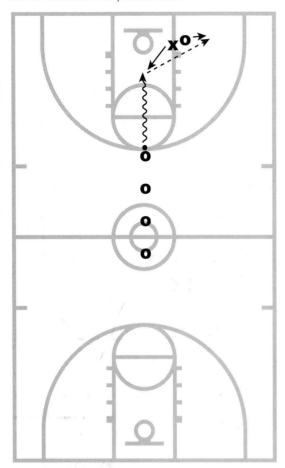

Drive and Dish.

them out loud) before she dribbles by the defender (who lets her go by). When she comes to the next defender, she comes to a jump stop and pivots for another 3 seconds (again counting out loud). She uses a curl pass to pass around the defender to the fourth player in the line. Curl passes are the only passes allowed. After this sequence, the original passer goes to guard the player she just passed to, and the drill continues.

Emphasis: Encourage passers to use ball fakes to set up the pass and to rip the ball through with their elbows out.

26. Drive and Dish

This 2-on-1 drill works on dribble penetration and help defense. Set up a line of players on the right block and a ball line of players at the top of the circle. The first block player is on defense, and the second block player is on offense. The first player in the ball line drives to the basket (the assumption is she's beaten her defender). As she enters the lane, the block defender comes out to defend against the basket. If she arrives in time, the dribbler *dishes the ball*—makes a bounce pass to the other offensive player, who should be open for a layup or short jump shot. The three players play 2-on-1 until a score or the defender gets the ball. Then the defender goes to the ball line, the offensive block player becomes the defender, the dribbler goes to the block line, and the drill continues.

Variation: Add a perimeter defender. She lets the dribbler drive by but then recovers to guard her man. The players play 2-on-2 until a score or the defense gets the ball.

Moving without the Ball Drills

27. V-Cut

The players form two lines at the wings with two passers at the top of the circle. The first player in each line has a ball.

 The drill begins when each wing passes to the passer on her side of the court. She cuts to the block, makes a swim move and V-cut, and cuts back to the perimeter. The passer leads her with the ball so the player has to keep coming to catch it. When she catches it, she squares up and gets in the triple threat position. Then she dribbles to the basket for a layup and gets her own rebound. After passing to the next player in her line, the player goes to the end of the other line.

 After each player has gone through each line twice, replace the passers so they can run the drill.

 Variation: After your players have the footwork and timing down, add a defender (see Wing Denial, Drill 49).

 Emphasis: Remind players to make a V-cut, not an I-cut. They should hold their lead hand out as a target.

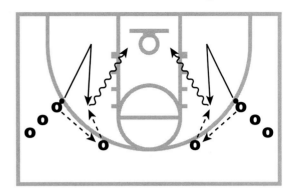

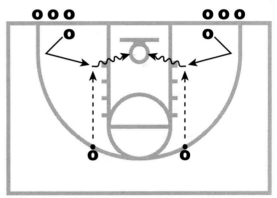

V-Cut (top).

Backdoor Cut (bottom).

28. Backdoor Cut

Have two lines, one in each short corner, and two passers at the 3-point arc above the elbows. Each passer has a ball. The drill starts when the first player in each line cuts toward the perimeter. After a few steps, the player plants her outside foot and makes a backdoor cut to the basket. The passer times her pass so the cutter can take one dribble and shoot a layup. The cutter retrieves her rebound, passes back to the passer, and goes to the end of the opposite line. As the cutter retrieves her rebound, the second player in line starts her cut.

29. Give-and-Go

Have two lines, one at each wing, and two passers at the top of the circle. The first player in each line has a ball. The drill starts when the first player in the wing line passes to the passer (the *give*). She immediately cuts to the basket (the *go*) for the return pass and the layup.

 Variation: Set up two passers, one at each wing, and a line at the top of the circle. The first two players in line have a ball. The first player passes to the right wing and cuts to the basket, with her lead hand extended. After she catches the ball, she shoots a layup. As she shoots, the second player in

Give-and-Go. Cutting from the wing (right). Cutting from the top of the circle (below).

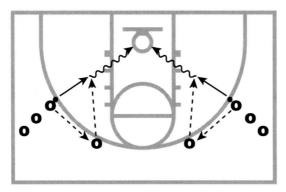

line passes to the left wing and repeats the give-and-go. As a change of pace, have the cutters pull up for a short jump shot.

Emphasis: The player should explode to the basket. She shouldn't go at half-speed, waiting for the passer to throw the ball. It's up to the passer to time the pass properly.

30. Screen Away

Have three lines, one at each wing and one at the top of the circle. The first two players in the top line each have a ball. The first player passes to the right wing and screens for the left wing, who cuts off the screener's shoulder into the lane to receive the pass from the right wing. She drives for a layup, retrieves the rebound, and passes to the next player in the top line. Meanwhile, as the player shoots her layup, the next group of three players begin the sequence with the player at the top of the circle passing to the player on the right wing.

After each sequence, the players change lines. Once every player has done the drill twice from each position, the player at the top passes to the left wing and screens for the right wing.

Variation: Once the players are comfortable doing this drill, add three defenders.

Emphasis: Remind players to wait for the screen, wait for the screen, and wait for the screen.

Screen Away.

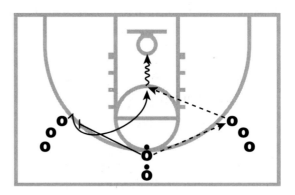

Shooting Drills

31. Floor Follow-Through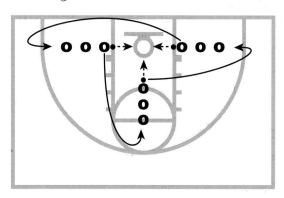

Each player is on her back on the floor, with a ball in her shooting hand, ready to shoot. The player snaps her wrist, practicing her follow-through and catching the ball when it comes down.

This drill can be done at home. As homework, you might want to assign twenty-five floor shots a night before bedtime.

Emphasis: As the ball rolls off the players' fingertips, they should make sure it has backspin.

32. Chair Follow-Through

Place a chair 3 feet in front of the basket. A player sits in it with her back straight and shoots at the basket. Since she can't use her legs to get the ball to the basket, she has to have a good follow-through with maximum arm extension. This drill helps correct common problems such as "short-arming" the shot and not snapping the wrist enough. As the player shoots, have a second player catch the ball out of the basket and hand it to her, so that the shooter can maintain her position in the chair. Switch players after ten shots. This drill takes little time and is well worth the time. My players believe it has improved their shooting.

Variation: If you have multiple baskets in the gym, place chairs at every basket, divide your team into small groups, and have them compete against each other. For example, each team shoots for 2 minutes or until a team makes fifty shots.

33. Warm-Up Shooting

The importance of starting in close to the basket when your players begin to work on shooting cannot be overemphasized. How can a player expect to make 15-footers if she can't make 5-footers?

Each player starts on the right block, focusing on the fundamentals, such as balance, arm extension, and good follow-through. After she makes five shots, she shoots from in front of the basket. After making five shots from there, she shoots from the left block. By starting in close, the player gains confidence in her shot and warms up for longer shots. After she competes that sequence, she's ready to step out to 8 to 10 feet from the basket and start again.

Three-Line Form Shooting.

34. Three-Line Form Shooting

Set up three lines, one at each block and one in front of the basket. Each player has a ball. The first player in the line on the right side shoots a bank shot and retrieves her rebound. As she does, the first player in the middle line shoots and retrieves her rebound, followed by the first player in the line on the left side. After a player retrieves her rebound, she rotates counterclockwise to the next line.

Players get only one shot. If a player misses, she doesn't take another shot until it's her turn again. Once your players get the hang of it, this drill has the players shooting a lot of shots in a short time. As they improve, have them step back to a distance of 8 to 10 feet and keep going.

Emphasis: Players should check their feet before shooting. Are they in the right position? Have them hold their follow-through long enough to make sure their arm is straight. Players shooting in front of the basket shouldn't shoot a bank shot.

35. Two-Line Shooting

Set up two lines on the second hash mark along each side of the lane, facing each other. The first two players in the right line have a ball. The drill begins when the first player passes across the lane to the first player in the left line. That player steps toward the pass with her left foot and pivots into the shot. As the shooter retrieves her rebound, the second player in the right line passes to the second player in the left line. The drill continues, with all the players in line passing or shooting. After 2 minutes, switch the balls to the left line, and have the players in the right line step into the pass with their right foot. After 2 minutes, move the lines out to the elbows and repeat the drill.

Variation: As your players get the footwork down, you can add a lot to this drill, such as a pump fake and one dribble to the right, a pump fake and one dribble to the left, ball fakes, and a one-dribble drive to the hoop.

Emphasis: Players should give the passer a target and should catch the ball in a crouch so they're ready to shoot after they pivot.

36. Shooting off the Pass

Start with two cutter lines in the short corners and two passers above the elbows. The first player in the cutter line makes a V-cut to the perimeter and holds her hand out as a target for the passer. When she catches the ball, she pivots on her inside foot, squares up, and shoots. As she retrieves her rebound (one shot only), the second player in line starts her cut. After shooting, each player goes to the end of the other line.

Variation: The players can make a shot fake, take one dribble, and shoot. They can also make a shot fake and drive. Switch the cutter lines to the wings, then to the top of the circle.

Emphasis: Remind players not to rush. They should always square up into the triple threat position when they catch the ball on the perimeter.

37. Spot Shooting

Players like this fun drill. Divide the players into two teams and set up each team in a line at a block. The first player in each line has a ball. On your signal, the player shoots, retrieves her rebound (whether made or missed), passes to the next player in her line, and goes to the back of her line. Each team keeps track of their made shots, shouting the number when another shot scores ("Twelve!"). The first line to reach twenty-five baskets wins.

Variation: Each team shoots five shots from six spots: the right block, midway up the lane line, the elbow, the other elbow, the other midway point, and the left block. The first team to "go around the world" wins.

Emphasis: Players should focus on shooting with good form and not rush because they're in a hurry to score. They'll score more points when they shoot with good form.

38. Game Shots 📣

Emphasize practicing *game shots*, shots the players will take in games. Every player has spots on the floor where she's most comfortable shooting. I define game shots as being shots that an unguarded player will make at least 60 percent of the time. Lower this figure to match your players' skills.

Have your players shoot game shots from various spots on the floor, not moving from one spot to the next until they've made five shots at the first spot. After they've finished, have them repeat the sequence, this time with a pump fake and dribble.

39. Knockout 📣

One of the most fun shooting drills is called "Knockout" or "Gotcha." You can do this drill with as few as two players, but the more shooters you have, the more fun it is. The players form a line at the free throw line (if your girls are beginners, start them closer to the basket). The first two players in line each have a ball. The first player shoots a free throw and follows her shot. If she makes it, she retrieves the ball and passes it to the next person in line without a ball. If she misses, she gets her own rebound and tries to score from wherever she gets the rebound before the second player scores. The second player can shoot as soon as the first player leaves the free throw line. If the second player scores before the first player does, the first player is out and leaves the game. The drill continues until one player remains.

40. Beat the Star 📣

This drill has two players and a ball. One player is the shooter, and the other is the rebounder. The shooter picks an imaginary player to shoot against (such as Michael Jordan or Diana Taurasi). The shooter takes game shots, moving to a new spot after each shot. Every made shot counts as 1 point for the player, and every miss counts as 1 point for the star player. The player continues shooting until either she or the star player reaches 10 points. The shooter and the rebounder trade places and repeat the drill.

41. One Ball, Two Players 📣

The drill begins with one player under the basket with a ball and another player somewhere on the perimeter. The first player passes to the shooter, who catches the ball and shoots. As she does, the passer runs to a spot on the floor where she wants to receive the ball. The shooter rebounds her shot (whether made or missed), passes to the new shooter, and runs out to another spot. Run this drill for 2 minutes or until one set of shooters makes a certain number of shots.

This drill is a good conditioner and teaches players to follow their shots. You can award extra points if a shooter catches the shot (whether made or missed) before it hits the floor. I have my players call their partner's name as they wait for the pass. This reinforces the habit of calling for the ball in games when they're open.

Variation: Have the passer run at the shooter with a hand up to contest the shot, so the shooter will get used to defensive pressure. Add moves with the shot, such as one or two dribbles, or have the shooters drive to the basket for a layup.

42. Two Balls, Three Players

This is an excellent drill that my teams use often. It works on game shots, conditioning, following shots, rebounding, and passing. Set up three players at various shooting spots on the floor. Two players have balls, and one player begins the drill by shooting. She follows her shot, rebounds, passes to the player without a ball, and runs to a new spot. Meanwhile, the second player shoots and follows the same sequence, resulting in an active nonstop drill. The players keep track of the made shots. Each player who scores shouts the new number of made shots. Run this drill for 2 minutes or until one trio scores a certain number of points.

Variation: As with One Ball, Two Players (Drill 41), you can add moves with the ball or drives, or you can designate a certain number of shots from certain spots on the court. As your players become familiar with the drill, adjust it to best meet the needs of your team.

43. Two-Line Layups

This is the standard half-court drill many teams use to warm up. Set up two lines above the 3-point arc at a 45-degree angle to the basket. The first three players in the right line have a ball. As the first player dribbles to the basket to shoot a right-handed layup, the first person in the other line comes in to rebound the shot (whether made or missed). After the shot, the dribbler runs to the rebound line. The rebounder dribbles to the corner, passes to an open player in the dribbler line, and runs to the back of the line. After each player shoots several layups, switch the balls to the other line. The dribblers now shoot left-handed layups.

Variation: Add a pass. The player in the right line dribbles in, comes to a jump stop at the edge of the lane, and makes a bounce pass to the other player, who shoots a left-handed layup. Add a jump shot. Instead of shooting layups, the players pull up for an 8- to 10-foot shot.

44. Full-Court Layups

Set up two lines, a ball line at the left elbow (as viewed from the baseline) and a cutter line at the right elbow. The lines face the far basket, and every player in the ball line has a ball. The first player in the ball line speed dribbles straight down the court as the first player in the cutter line sprints straight down the court. When the dribbler reaches the opposite elbow, she comes to a jump stop and makes a bounce pass to the cutter, who shoots a layup. The dribbler gets the rebound and speed dribbles back down the right side of the court to the baseline and passes to the cutter, who has sprinted down the court on the left side to the baseline. The cutter goes to the end of the ball line, and the dribbler goes to the end of the cutter line. As each pair reaches the far elbows, the next pair begins. Switch the ball to the right line after a few minutes or after a certain number of made layups.

Variation: This is a good warm-up drill if run at three-quarter speed.

45. Foul Shots

Your team should practice foul shots at every practice. The more baskets you have, the better, but even if you have only two baskets, don't ignore this crucial part of the game. Many games are won or lost at the free throw line.

The simplest drill is to divide your players into pairs at the baskets and have each player shoot ten free throws, while the rebounder keeps track of the made shots. We record our players' shooting at every practice so we can chart their progress during the season.

46. Three-Player Foul Shots

This is a good drill when you have enough baskets to divide your players into three-person teams. Each team designates a shooter, a rebounder, and a runner. As the shooter and rebounder stay at the basket, the runner runs a lap. When she finishes, she goes to the free throw line and replaces the shooter, who becomes the new rebounder. The previous rebounder becomes the new runner. As the players tire, they'll learn how to make foul shots in game conditions. Stop the drill after a certain number of made shots or after a certain length of time.

Defensive Drills

47. Defensive Slides

Stand in front of the basket with three lines of players facing you; the first line goes along the free throw line extended. There should be 3 to 4 feet between players. Have the players get into a defensive on-ball stance. When you point to either sideline, the players step-slide in that direction until you point in the other direction. When you point behind you, players make an advance step, and when you point behind them, they make a retreat step. Do this for 30 seconds at a time, changing signals in a random pattern. After a 15-second pause, go for another 30 seconds. As the season progresses, extend the time to what the players can handle.

48. Slide the Court

Line up your players at one corner of the court. The first player faces the near lane area. When the drill starts, the player step-slides to the near elbow, makes a swing step so she now faces the near sideline, and step-slides to the midcourt corner. When she arrives there, she sprints to the other sideline. Then, facing that sideline, she step-slides to the other elbow, makes a swing step, and continues to the corner. She goes to the back of the line. When the first player reaches the near elbow, the second player begins the drill. When the second player reaches the near elbow, the third player begins, and so on.

Variation: In the full-court version of this drill, the players follow the same path they used when doing Zigzag Dribbling (Drill 18).

49. Wing Denial

Set up two lines at each wing and two passers above the 3-point line at the top of the circle. Put eight or more balls next to the passers and designate several *shaggers* (players who collect balls that are caught or batted away). The first player in each line is the defender, and the second player is the cutter. As the cutter heads toward the block, the defender step-slides in a denial stance, looking at the ball over her shoulder. The cutter makes a swim move, V-cuts, and cuts to the perimeter. Whether or not the cutter is open, the passer throws the pass. If the cutter is open, she catches the ball, passes it to a shagger, and cuts again. If the defender is in position, she deflects the ball with her outstretched hand. The cutter and defender go back and forth several times, and the passer passes every time the cutter comes out for the ball.

Variation: Add a 1-on-1 element. When the cutter catches the ball, she squares up and drives

Slide the Court.

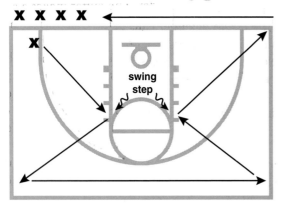

on the defender. As your players get better at this drill, limit the number of dribbles (two or three) they can take when driving to the basket.

Emphasis: The defender should use her hand nearest the ball to deflect it. Too often, players try to steal the ball using both hands. It takes an extra split second to turn their bodies, and they're often too late. Their momentum takes them beyond the cutter, who's now open for a drive.

50. One-on-One Half-Court Drive

Set up one line at midcourt with a ball. The first player is the defender, and the second player is the offensive player. The offensive player must check the ball. She then tries to drive to the basket. The defender works on cutting her off with step-slides and tries to disrupt what the offensive player wants to do. When the offensive player shoots, the defender blocks her out. They play until the offensive player scores or the defender has the ball. The offensive player then goes to the end of the line. The defender stays on defense until she's made three defensive stops. After she's made the third stop, the current offensive player becomes the new defender.

51. Two-on-Two Defensive Play

Have four players play 2-on-2 at each basket, guarding each other man-to-man. They can either be guards against guards, posts against posts, or a guard and a post against a guard and a post. The offensive team can do what it wants (no set plays). When a team scores, the other team takes the ball out at the top of the circle. Set a time limit or a score limit. When the limit is reached, rotate the teams so every team plays against every other team.

Variation: Run a 3-on-3 drill or a 4-on-4 drill .

Emphasis: Tell your players not to lose sight of the ball and to be ready to help out the other defensive player.

52. Dribble Drive

This drill works on on-ball defense as well as closing out. Set up a line under the basket and put an offensive player at the free throw line. The first player in line rolls a ball to the offensive player and closes out on the player. The offensive player can't shoot. She must drive to the basket, using no more than three dribbles (two, if you have older players). The defender contests the drive and the shot. They play 1-on-1 until the offensive player scores or the defender gets control of the ball. If the offensive player scores, she plays against the next defender. If the defender makes a stop, she becomes the offensive player.

Emphasis: Defenders need to close out low, using choppy steps. They shouldn't leave their feet for shot fakes.

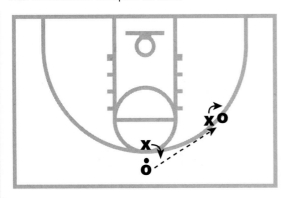

Pass to wing in the Two-Man Shell.

Shell Drills

53. Two-Man Shell

Start with the Two-Man Shell. Set up two offensive players, one at the top of the circle with a ball and one at the right wing, each guarded by a defender. The defender guarding the player with the ball is in the on-ball stance. The other defender is in the denial stance. The player with the ball passes to the wing. As the ball is in the air, the passer's defender switches to the denial stance, and the receiver's defender switches to the on-ball stance. Have them pass back and forth, the defenders jumping to the ball and switching positions. Each time the defenders jump to a new position, they should shout the name of their new position. "Ball, ball ball!" or "Deny, deny, deny!"

54. Three-Man Shell

For the next level, add a third offensive player at the other wing and a third defender. At the start the drill, the defender guarding the player with the ball should be in the on-ball stance, and the other two defenders should be in denial stances.

The drill begins when the player with the ball passes to the right wing. The right wing's defender switches to the on-ball stance, the passer's defender switches to the denial stance, and the left wing's defender switches from the denial stance to the help-side stance (her man is two passes away). Since the ball is above the free throw line extended, the help-side defender has a foot in the lane.

Have the right wing make a skip pass to the left wing. Her defender should switch to a help-side stance, the defender at the top should go from a denial stance on one side of the offensive player to a denial stance on the other

Skip pass in the Three-Man Shell.

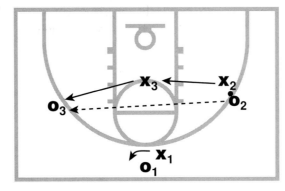

Helping on the drive in the Three-Man Shell.

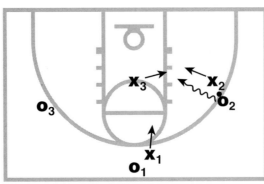

side. The right wing's defender should switch from the on-ball stance to a help-side position.

Each time a player makes a pass, the receiver should hold the ball until you're satisfied the defenders are in the right positions. As the defenders get better at the drill, have the passers pass after a count of two. As your defenders improve, have the passers throw the ball after a count of one.

The next step in the progression is to add *help defense*. As the players execute the drill, whenever you call "Drive," the player with the ball immediately drives by her defender, who makes no attempt to stay with her. The other defenders practice dropping into the lane to stop the drive.

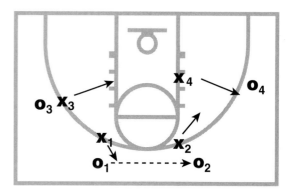

Four-Man Shell.

55. Four-Man Shell 👉

Once your players become skilled at the two- and three-player drills, add another offensive player and another defender. Set up two offensive players on the 3-point arc at the elbow areas and two offensive players on the wings. Follow the same progression as in the Three-Man Shell.

56. Five-Man Shell 👉

For the Five-Man Shell, add a post player at the high post and a fifth defender. Once the players get good at this, vary the five-man setup to mirror the offensive setups your team uses, such as the 3-out, 2-in formation.

Rebounding Drills

57. Touch the Ball

Put a ball in the middle of the center circle area. Have four players stand in the circle, facing out, equidistant from each other. Have four other players stand outside the circle area, each directly across the line from a player inside the line. At your signal, the players inside the circle block out the outside players, while the outside players try to get around them to touch the ball. The goal is for the players blocking out to keep their opponents away from the ball for 3 seconds. Once they do that, the drill is over, and the next group of players repeats the drill. Make sure you match up players of similar height.

If you coach older players, have only two pairs of players go at one time to avoid the possibility of players colliding as they go for the ball.

58. Line Rebounding

Set up pairs of players on the free throw line extended. The players closest to the basket are defenders and face the other players, who are offensive players but don't have a ball. On your signal, the defenders pivot and block out their man. The offensive players try to get around them.

Emphasis: Each defender should stay low, make contact, and use choppy steps to keep the player she's guarding on her back.

59. Three-on-Three Rebounding

This drill works on defensive positioning and rebounding. Set up three offensive players, two outside the blocks and one player 6 feet in front of the basket. Assign three defenders to them. As you or an assistant dribbles the ball, the defenders adjust their positions (the offensive players don't move). Then shoot the ball. The defenders block out as the offensive players try to get around them. If an offensive player gets the rebound, she puts it back up. Play continues until there's a score or the defense has the ball. Every defensive rebound counts as 1 point, and every offensive rebound counts as 2 points. After running the drill five times, switch the offense and the defense.

Fast-Break Drills

60. One-on-Zero Fast Break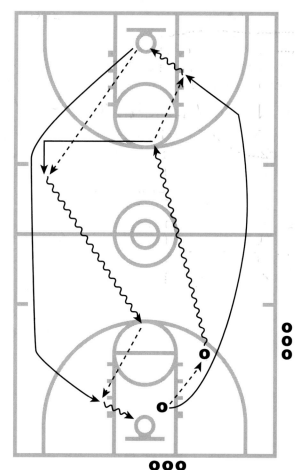

Set up two lines, a rebound line under the basket and an outlet line in the free throw line extended area. The first player in the rebound line throws the ball off the backboard, jumps for the rebound, chins it, pivots away from the middle of the lane, and throws a two-hand outlet pass to the first player in the outlet line (who shouts "Outlet!" to let the player know where she is). That player then speed dribbles to the opposite basket for a layup. After she grabs her own rebound, she dribbles to the near basket and shoots another layup. The rebounder and the outlet player switch lines. When each outlet player catches the ball, the next rebounder starts the drill.

61. Outlet Layups

Set up two lines as in the One-on-Zero Fast Break. This time, the first four players in the rebound line have a ball. The first player throws the ball against the backboard to create a rebound. She rebounds, pivots, and throws an outlet pass to the first player in the outlet line. While the outlet player speed dribbles to the top of the opposite circle, the rebounder runs the right lane, which was vacated by the outlet player. The rebounder sprints to the free throw line extended and cuts to the basket.

When the dribbler reaches the top of the circle, she comes to a jump stop and passes (with a bounce pass) to the cutter. After the cutter makes a layup, she rebounds the ball and passes it to the dribbler, who has sprinted to a new outlet position on the left side of the court (as viewed from the original baseline). They

Outlet Layups.

then run the drill going the other way. When they finish, each player goes to the end of the other line.

As the first rebounder/cutter crosses midcourt, the second pair begins the drill. There should be four pairs of players running the drill at the same time. After 2 to 3 minutes, change the lines so the outlet line is on the left half of the court, as viewed from the baseline. Now the players work on shooting left-handed layups at each basket.

62. Two-on-One Fast Break

Set up two lines at midcourt, a ball line on the left and a cutter line on the right, each halfway between the center circle and the sideline. The first two players in the ball line have a ball. Put a defender at the free throw line. The first player in the ball line dribbles hard toward the basket as the first player in the cutter line runs the right lane. When the defender comes over to guard the dribbler, the dribbler comes to a jump stop and passes to the cutter. The cutter should have an easy layup. If the cutter misses the layup, the group plays 2-on-1 until the offense scores, the defender gets the ball, or the ball goes out-of-bounds. After they're finished, the defender runs out to defend the next pair, and the dribbler and the cutter switch lines.

In a 2-on-1 fast break, the dribbler should dribble at the nearest elbow. This creates good offensive spacing. If the dribbler goes to the middle of the free throw line, the defender will be closer to the cutter and more able to defend both players. When the dribbler heads to the elbow away from the cutter, the defender has to choose whether to guard the dribbler or the cutter. A defender's first priority is always to stop the ball. If she cheats toward the cutter in anticipation of a pass, the dribbler should drive to the basket.

Once the defender has defended against every offensive pair, she joins one of the lines, and another defender replaces her. After every player has played defense, switch the balls to the other line.

63. Three-on-Two Fast Break

Set up three lines at midcourt, a ball line in the middle and two cutter lines next to the sidelines. Put a defender at the free throw line and a defender in front of the basket. The first player in the ball line dribbles hard to the basket. The dribbler should head to the middle of the lane on a 3-on-2 break, as opposed to heading to the elbow on a 2-on-1 break. The first player in each cutter line runs her lane, heading straight at the baseline. The play-

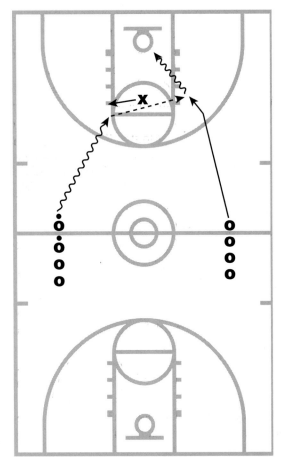

Two-on-One.

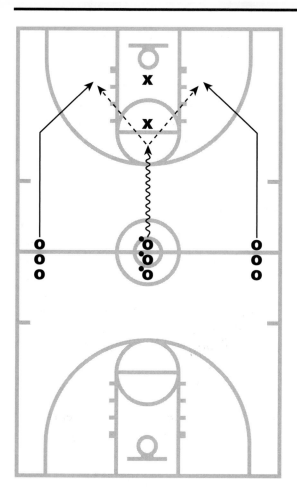

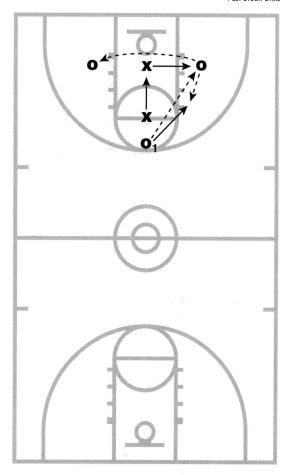

ers cut to the basket when they reach the free throw line extended. The front defender stops the ball so the dribbler can't penetrate into the lane. This forces her to come to a jump stop and pass to one of the cutters.

She *follows the pass* by going to the elbow nearest the player to whom she passed. The back defender waits until a pass is made. When the ball's in the air, she sprints to the receiver to guard her. As she does this, the front defender drops down to the basket to prevent a pass from the receiver to the opposite cutter for an easy layup. The cutter who received the ball has several options:

- pass to the opposite cutter, if she's open
- drive, if the defender isn't in a good on-ball position
- shoot, if she's open
- pass back to the dribbler at the elbow

If the cutter passes back to the dribbler, the dribbler can drive, shoot, or pass to the other cutter. At this point it's important to shoot, because the rest of the defense will be back.

**Three-on-Two Fast Break.
Part 1 (left). Part 2 (right).**

After each pair of defenders has defended against every offensive trio, replace them with new defenders. Run the drill until everyone has played defense.

64. Three-on-Two, Two-on-One

Don't try this drill until your players are familiar with the Two-on-One Fast Break (Drill 62) and the Three-on-Two Fast Break (Drill 63). Set up three lines along the baseline and two defenders at the far basket, one in front of the basket and the other at the free throw line. The first three players in the lines head up the court on a 3-on-2 fast break. They're limited to one shot. After the shot, no matter if it's made or missed, the shooter sprints back down the court to defend against the two defenders, who now become offensive players. The offensive players who didn't shoot stay at that basket and become defenders. After one shot at the 2-on-1, the next player in the middle line grabs the made or missed shot and starts another 3-on-2 break.

Three-on-Two, Two-on-One. 3-on-2 action (left). 2-on-1 action (right).

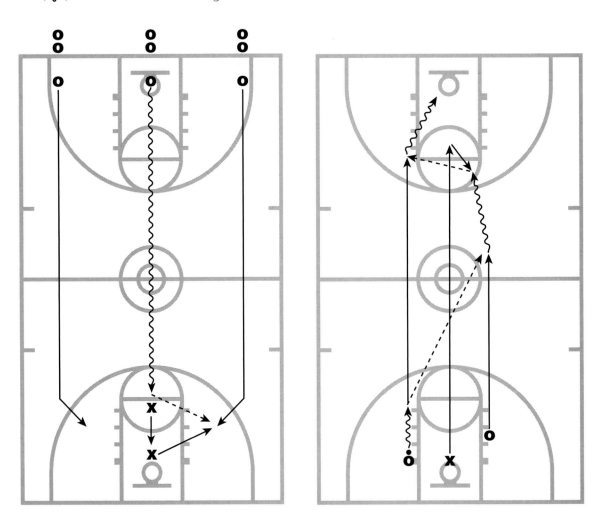

65. Three-on-Three-on-Three 👉

Split your players into teams of three. Assuming you have four teams, pick two to start play. The other two will each be under a basket with a ball, ready to come into the game. The teams play full-court man-to-man defense. When a team scores, it leaves the court and is replaced by the team under the basket where the score occurred. The new team inbounds the ball. When a team is scored on, it stays on defense. This is a full-throttle, tiring drill that works on the fast break and all other phases of the game.

Variation: Add a limited-dribble rule, so that the players are limited to, for example, one dribble. This forces the player with the ball to be patient, to see the court, and to make better passes. It also forces her teammates to work harder to get open.

APPENDIX
Sample Tryout Evaluation Sheet

NAME _____ Height____ Position_____

Physical: Timed sprint (up and back)_____ Timed dribble (up and back) _____

Conditioning:* _____

Mental:* Hustle_____ Aggressiveness_____ Toughness_____ Attitude_____

Ball-handling:* Strong hand dribble_____ Weak hand dribble _____ Eyes up_____

Control dribble_____ Speed dribble_____ Crossover_____

Passing:* Weave drill _____ Outlet drill _____ Scrimmages_____

Shooting: Right hand layups_____ Left hand layups_____

Free throws (best of 10)_____ Jump shots (1 minute)_____

Offense:* 1 on 1_____ Getting open_____ Court savvy_____

Rebounding:* _____

Defense:* Overall_____ Stance_____ Positioning_____ Intensity_____

Comments: _____

_____

Player made team_____ yes _____ no

Evaluator_____ Date_____

* Rate from 1-5

Sample End-of-Tryouts Letter

Dear_____,

Thank you for trying out for the Shady Branch 6th Grade Team. We're sorry to tell you we didn't choose you for the team. We wish we could make room for everyone who tried out, but we have room for only twelve players.

It was a difficult decision, because you can be a good basketball player. It came down to the fact that you don't have the experience of some of the other players. Here's how we evaluated your skills:

Dribbling: OK, but you need to work on dribbling with your head up.

Passing: Good. You made a number of good passes in the scrimmages.

Shooting: Needs work, particularly your layups.

Defense: Good. You move your feet well.

Rebounding: Needs work. When you grow taller, you'll be a better rebounder!

Attitude: Very good. We really liked your enthusiasm!

We hope you won't let your disappointment stop you from playing basketball. It's a great sport, but it takes time to learn how to play. Thanks again for trying out.

Sincerely,

The Coach

Sample Player-Parent Handout

To: 6th Grade Basketball Players (and your parents)
From: The Coach

I'm excited to begin the season and am looking forward to coaching you!
These are our team rules and expectations:

1. **Equipment.** Wear shorts, a clean T-shirt, and basketball shoes to practice. Bring a water bottle as well as any medical equipment you need, such as an inhaler or an ankle or knee brace. Don't bring a ball.

2. **Punctuality.** Be on time. We have little gym time available, so it's important to take advantage of every minute.

3. **Absences.** When you play a team sport, you're committing to attend every practice and game. When you're absent, you miss a chance to improve and help the team. If you miss the practice before a game, you can't play in that game. If you miss practice or a game for an "unexcused reason" (like choosing to play another sport), it will hurt your playing time in the next game.

4. **Effort.** Do your best every time you walk on the court. Your teammates and coaches are counting on you.

5. **Enthusiasm.** Bring a positive attitude, regardless of whether the team is winning or losing games. We expect players and parents to provide unconditional enthusiasm throughout the season.

6. **Respect, dignity, and tolerance.** Treat your teammates and coaches like you want them to treat you—with respect, dignity, and tolerance.

7. **Team player.** The team comes ahead of any person on the team. Do your best to help your teammates play better.

8. **Sportsmanship.** We expect you to display good sportsmanship. We'll talk about what that means during the season.

9. **Playing time.** You have to earn the right to play in games. If you work hard in practice and have a positive attitude, you'll play in every game. If you don't, you won't.

10. **Success.** Sure, we'll try to win as many games as possible, but that's not what makes for a successful season. The most important goals are to learn fundamental skills, to improve as a player and a team, to work as hard as we can, and to have fun. I have no doubt we'll achieve those goals!

If any of you have any questions or concerns, please call me at 111-1111 or e-mail me at imyourcoach@bball.hoops.
Did I mention how excited I am about the season?

Sample Master Practice Plan

FUNDAMENTAL SKILLS:

Offense

Jump stop

Triple threat

Pivoting: front pivot, rear pivot

Dribbling: strong hand, weak hand, control dribble, speed dribble, crossover

Moves without ball: V-cut, backdoor cut

Moves with ball: shot fakes, jab-and-go, jab-and-cross

Passing: bounce, chest, push, overhead, baseball, curl

Catching

Setting and using screens

Give-and-go

Pick-and-roll

Defense

Stance

Step-slides

Advance step, retreat step, swing step

On-ball defense

Denial defense

Help-side defense

Trapping

Fouling intentionally

Rebounding: blocking out

Shooting

Proper form

Free throws

Layups

Shooting off the pass and the dribble

TEAM SKILLS:

Offense

Give-and-Go Offense

Screen-Away Offense

One-Guard Offense

Two-Guard Offense

2-on-1 fast break

3-on-2 fast break

Sideline Stack Play

Man-to-man inbounds play: Box Man Play

Zone inbounds play: Box Zone Play

V Press Break

Defense

Half court: man-to-man, 2-3 zone

Full court: man-to-man

Sample Daily Practice Plan

Time	Minutes	Activity	Emphasis
2:00	8	Warm-ups: Full-court layups Slide the Court (Drill 48)	Stay low
	2	Stretching	
2:10	10	Ball handling: Stationary dribbling Zigzag Dribbling (Drill 18)	Keep head up
2:20	8	Passing: Pairs Monkey in the Middle (Drill 20)	No overhead passes
2:28	2	Water break	
2:30	5	Form shooting	
	5	Triangle shooting	Check follow-through
2:40	10	Pairs shooting (two at a basket)	
2:50	8	Layups	
2:58	2	Water break	
3:00	10	1-on-1 defense	Blocking out
3:10	10	Three-Man Shell (Drill 54)	Help-side defense
3:20	8	3-on-3 half court (two baskets)	
3:28	2	Water break	
3:30	10	Two-Guard Offense	Ball movement
3:40	15	5-on-5 full court	
3:55	5	Wrap-up talk	Saturday's game

Sample Stat Sheet

Opponent:_____ Where:_____ Date:_____

Score: 1st QTR_____ 2nd QTR_____ 3rd QTR_____ 4th QTR_____

Fouls	Player	Off Rebs	Def Rebs	Assists	Steals	Turnovers	Blocks
123 45		1 2 3 4 5 6 7 8 9 10 11 12 13 14 15	1 2 3 4 5 6 7 8 9 10 11 12 13 14 15	1 2 3 4 5 6 7 8 9 10 11 12 13	1 2 3 4 5 6 7 8 9 10 11	1 2 3 4 5 6 7 8 9 10 11 12 13	1 2 3 4 5 6
123 45		1 2 3 4 5 6 7 8 9 10 11 12 13 14 15	1 2 3 4 5 6 7 8 9 10 11 12 13 14 15	1 2 3 4 5 6 7 8 9 10 11 12 13	1 2 3 4 5 6 7 8 9 10 11	1 2 3 4 5 6 7 8 9 10 11 12 13	1 2 3 4 5 6
123 45		1 2 3 4 5 6 7 8 9 10 11 12 13 14 15	1 2 3 4 5 6 7 8 9 10 11 12 13 14 15	1 2 3 4 5 6 7 8 9 10 11 12 13	1 2 3 4 5 6 7 8 9 10 11	1 2 3 4 5 6 7 8 9 10 11 12 13	1 2 3 4 5 6
123 45		1 2 3 4 5 6 7 8 9 10 11 12 13 14 15	1 2 3 4 5 6 7 8 9 10 11 12 13 14 15	1 2 3 4 5 6 7 8 9 10 11 12 13	1 2 3 4 5 6 7 8 9 10 11	1 2 3 4 5 6 7 8 9 10 11 12 13	1 2 3 4 5 6
123 45		1 2 3 4 5 6 7 8 9 10 11 12 13 14 15	1 2 3 4 5 6 7 8 9 10 11 12 13 14 15	1 2 3 4 5 6 7 8 9 10 11 12 13	1 2 3 4 5 6 7 8 9 10 11	1 2 3 4 5 6 7 8 9 10 11 12 13	1 2 3 4 5 6
123 45		1 2 3 4 5 6 7 8 9 10 11 12 13 14 15	1 2 3 4 5 6 7 8 9 10 11 12 13 14 15	1 2 3 4 5 6 7 8 9 10 11 12 13	1 2 3 4 5 6 7 8 9 10 11	1 2 3 4 5 6 7 8 9 10 11 12 13	1 2 3 4 5 6
123 45		1 2 3 4 5 6 7 8 9 10 11 12 13 14 15	1 2 3 4 5 6 7 8 9 10 11 12 13 14 15	1 2 3 4 5 6 7 8 9 10 11 12 13	1 2 3 4 5 6 7 8 9 10 11	1 2 3 4 5 6 7 8 9 10 11 12 13	1 2 3 4 5 6
123 45		1 2 3 4 5 6 7 8 9 10 11 12 13 14 15	1 2 3 4 5 6 7 8 9 10 11 12 13 14 15	1 2 3 4 5 6 7 8 9 10 11 12 13	1 2 3 4 5 6 7 8 9 10 11	1 2 3 4 5 6 7 8 9 10 11 12 13	1 2 3 4 5 6
123 45		1 2 3 4 5 6 7 8 9 10 11 12 13 14 15	1 2 3 4 5 6 7 8 9 10 11 12 13 14 15	1 2 3 4 5 6 7 8 9 10 11 12 13	1 2 3 4 5 6 7 8 9 10 11	1 2 3 4 5 6 7 8 9 10 11 12 13	1 2 3 4 5 6
123 45		1 2 3 4 5 6 7 8 9 10 11 12 13 14 15	1 2 3 4 5 6 7 8 9 10 11 12 13 14 15	1 2 3 4 5 6 7 8 9 10 11 12 13	1 2 3 4 5 6 7 8 9 10 11	1 2 3 4 5 6 7 8 9 10 11 12 13	1 2 3 4 5 6
123 45		1 2 3 4 5 6 7 8 9 10 11 12 13 14 15	1 2 3 4 5 6 7 8 9 10 11 12 13 14 15	1 2 3 4 5 6 7 8 9 10 11 12 13	1 2 3 4 5 6 7 8 9 10 11	1 2 3 4 5 6 7 8 9 10 11 12 13	1 2 3 4 5 6
123 45		1 2 3 4 5 6 7 8 9 10 11 12 13 14 15	1 2 3 4 5 6 7 8 9 10 11 12 13 14 15	1 2 3 4 5 6 7 8 9 10 11 12 13	1 2 3 4 5 6 7 8 9 10 11	1 2 3 4 5 6 7 8 9 10 11 12 13	1 2 3 4 5 6
123 45		1 2 3 4 5 6 7 8 9 10 11 12 13 14 15	1 2 3 4 5 6 7 8 9 10 11 12 13 14 15	1 2 3 4 5 6 7 8 9 10 11 12 13	1 2 3 4 5 6 7 8 9 10 11	1 2 3 4 5 6 7 8 9 10 11 12 13	1 2 3 4 5 6

TOTALS

Sample Scorebook Sheet

Courtesy Big Red Publications

Sample Game Sheet

Opponent:_____ Where:_____ Date:_____ Score:_____

Pre Game

Starters: Goals: Results:

1   1

2   2

3   3

4   4

5   5

Absent:_____ Sick, injured_____

Post Game Review

Them

Strengths:

Weaknesses:

Offensive tendencies:

Defensive tendencies:

Best players:

Us

What we did well:

What we did poorly:

Referee Signals
Official NFHS Basketball Signals

Glossary

Advance step: A step in which the defender's lead foot steps toward her man, and her back foot slides forward.

Air ball: A shot that hits only air—it misses the rim and the backboard.

Air pass: A pass that goes straight through the air to the receiver.

And one: The *free throw* awarded to a shooter who is fouled as she scores.

Assist: A pass thrown to a player who immediately scores.

Backcourt: The half of the court a team is defending. The opposite of the *frontcourt*. Also refers to a team's guards.

Backdoor cut: An offensive play in which a player on the perimeter steps away from the basket, drawing the defender with her, and suddenly cuts to the basket behind the defender for a pass. The opposite of a *V-cut*.

Back screen: An offensive play in which a player comes from the *low post* to set a *screen* for a player on the perimeter.

Ball fake: A sudden movement by the player with the ball intended to cause the defender to move in one direction, allowing the passer to pass in another direction. Also called "pass fake."

Ball reversal: Passing the ball from one side of the court to the other.

Ball screen: An offensive play in which a player sets a *screen* on the defender guarding the player with the ball.

Ball side: The half of the court (if the court is divided lengthwise) that the ball is on. Also called the "strong side." The opposite of the *help side*.

Bank shot: A shot that hits the backboard before hitting the rim or going through the net.

Baseball pass: A one-handed pass thrown like a baseball.

Baseline: See *end line*.

Baseline out-of-bounds play: The play used to return the ball to the court from outside the baseline along the opponent's basket.

Basket cut: A cut toward the basket.

Bench: Refers to substitutes sitting on the sideline, as well as to the bench they sit on.

Block: (1) A violation in which a defender steps in front of a dribbler but is still moving when they collide. Also called a "blocking foul." (2) To tip or deflect a shooter's shot, altering its flight so the shot misses. (3) The small painted square on the floor next to the basket just outside the lane.

Block out: See *box out*.

Bonus: A team is "in the bonus" when it accumulates seven or more team fouls in a half, giving the other team a *free throw* on each subsequent foul. Also called being "over the limit."

Bounce pass: A pass that bounces once before reaching the receiver.

Box-and-one: A combination defense in which four defenders play *zone* in a box formation and the fifth defender guards one player *man-to-man*.

Box out: To make contact with an opposing player to establish rebounding position between the player and the ball. Also called "block out."

Box set: A formation in which four players align themselves as the four corners of a box. Often used for *baseline out-of-bounds plays*.

Brick: A bad shot that clanks off the backboard or rim.

Bump the cutter: To step in the way of a cutter who is trying to *cut* to the ball for a pass.

Carrying the ball: A violation that occurs when a player dribbling the ball brings her hand underneath the ball and momentarily carries it. Also called "palming."

Center: (1) The position in which a player, usually the tallest player on the team, stays near the basket. (2) The player who plays that position.

Center circle: The painted circle at midcourt used for the opening *jump ball*.

Charge: (1) A violation in which a player with the ball runs into a defender who is standing still. Also called a "charging foul." (2) To commit that violation.

Chest pass: An air pass thrown from the passer's chest to a teammate's chest. It can be a one-handed or two-handed pass.

Combination defense: A defense that is part *man-to-man* and part *zone*. Also called a "junk defense."

Continuity offense: A sequence of player and ball movement that repeats until a good shot is created.

Control dribble: A dribble maneuver in which the player keeps her body between the defender's body and the ball.

Court savvy: A term describing a player who plays smart basketball.

Court vision: A term describing a player who sees and understands what all the other players on the court are doing. This usually leads to having *court savvy*.

Crossover dribble: A dribbling maneuver in which a player dribbles the ball in front of her body so she can change the ball from one hand to the other.

Cross screen: A movement in which a player *cuts* across the lane to *screen* for a teammate.

Curl pass: A low, one-handed pass made by stepping around the defender's leg and extending the throwing arm. Also called a "hook pass."

Cut: (1) A sudden running movement to get open for a pass. 2) To make such a move. Also called "flash."

Dead ball: A stoppage of play called by the referee.

Dead-ball foul: A foul committed while the clock is stopped and the ball is not in play.

Defensive rebound: A *rebound* made off a missed shot at the basket a team is defending.

Defensive slide: The quick "step-slide" movement a defender makes when closely guarding the dribbler.

Defensive stance: The stance used to play defense (knees bent, feet wide, arms out).

Defensive stop: Gaining possession of the ball before the offensive team scores.

Delay offense: An offense used to take more time with each possession.

Denial defense: A defense in which a defender tries to prevent her man from receiving a pass.

Denial stance: The stance used to play denial defense (body low, knees bent, hand and foot in the passing lane).

Deny the ball: To use a *denial stance* to keep the offensive player from receiving a pass.

Diamond-and-one: A combination defense in which four defenders play zone in a diamond formation and the fifth defender guards a specific offensive player man-to-man.

Double down: To drop from the perimeter, leaving one's man or zone, to *double-team* a *low post* player.

Double dribble: A violation in which a player picks up her dribble and starts to dribble again. A common occurrence with young players.

Double-teaming: A defense in which two defenders guard the same offensive player at the same time.

Down screen: A play in which a player comes down from the perimeter or *high post* area to set a *screen* for a player in the *low post* area.

Dribble: (1) To advance the ball by bouncing it on the floor. (2) The bounce of the ball caused by a player pushing the ball downward.

Drive: To attack the basket by dribbling hard at it.

Drop step: A *low post* move in which an offensive player with her back to the basket swings one leg around the defender and uses it as a *pivot foot* to gain inside position.

Dunk: A shot in which the player jumps high and throws the ball down through the basket. Also called a "slam," a "jam," and a "slam-dunk."

Elbow: The corner made by the intersection of the *free throw line* and the *lane* line. Each lane area has two elbows.

End line: The line that marks the playing boundary at each end of the court. Also called the "baseline."

Face up: See *square up*.

Fast break: A play in which a team gains possession of the ball (through a defensive rebound, steal, or made shot) and then pushes the ball toward the other basket as fast as possible, hoping to catch the other team off guard and score an easy shot.

Field goal: A 2-point or 3-point basket.

Filling the lanes: A *fast break* in which players from the offensive team run up the court in the right lane, the middle lane, and the left lane.

Flagrant foul: Excessive physical contact (punching, kicking, etc.).

Flash: See *cut*.

Forward: A position usually played by a tall, athletic player. A "small forward" or a "3" plays on the *wing*, and a *power forward* or a "4" plays in the *high* or *low post* area.

Foul: A violation of the rules.

Foul line: See *free throw line*.

Foul shot: See *free throw*.

Foul trouble: (1) Player foul trouble occurs when a player accumulates three or four fouls and is in danger of fouling out. (2) Team foul trouble occurs when a team accumulates seven or more team fouls in a half and is "in the bonus."

Free throw: An uncontested shot taken from the free throw line as a result of a foul. Also called a "foul shot." A successful free throw is worth 1 point.

Free throw line: The line behind which a player stands to shoot a free throw. Also called the "foul line."

Free throw line extended: An imaginary line extending from the end of the *free throw line* to the *sidelines*.

Front: To guard a player by standing directly in front of her and therefore between her and the ball.

Frontcourt: A team's offensive half of the court. The opposite of the *backcourt*. Also refers to a team's *center* and *forwards*.

Full-court press: A *man-to-man* or *zone* defense in which the players guard the other team in the frontcourt. Also called a "press."

Give-and-go: An offensive play in which the player with the ball passes (*gives*) to a teammate and cuts (*goes*) to the basket to receive a return pass. One of the game's basic plays.

Goaltending: A violation in which a defender touches a shot as it nears the basket in a downward flight.

Guard: (1) A position on the perimeter. The *point guard* or "1" brings the ball up the court and begins the offense. The *shooting guard* or "2" is usually the team's best outside shooter. (2) To defend an offensive player closely.

Half-court line: The line at the center of the court parallel to the sidelines that divides the court in half. Also called the "midcourt line."

Hand-check: To make hand contact with a dribbler while guarding her.

Held ball: A situation in which two players hold the ball in their hands simultaneously, but neither can pull it away from the other. Also called a *jump ball*.

Help and recover: A defensive move in which a defender leaves her assigned player to guard a teammate's assigned player and then goes back to guard her own player.

Help side: The half of the court (if the court is divided lengthwise) that the ball is not on. Also called the "weak side." The opposite of the *ball side*.

Hesitation dribble: A dribbling maneuver in which the dribbler hesitates, pretending to pick up her dribble, but suddenly continues to the basket. Also called a "stop-and-go dribble."

High post: The area around the *free throw line*.

Hook pass: See *curl pass*.

Hook shot: A one-hand shot taken with a sweeping, windmill motion.

Hoop: The basket or rim.

Hoops: Slang term for the game of basketball.

Hops: A term used to describe how high a player can jump, as in "Eileen has great hops."

Inbound: To pass the ball to a teammate on the court from out-of-bounds.

Inbounder: The player who inbounds the ball.

Inside-out dribble: An advanced dribbling move, a fake crossover dribble.

Intentional foul: A foul that occurs when a player makes illegal contact with an opposing player without intending to get the ball.

Isolation play: An offensive play designed to have a specific player attack the basket 1-on-1. Also called "iso play."

Jab-and-cross: A play in which the offensive player makes a *jab step* in one direction and then follows it by driving by the defender on the other side.

Jab-and-go: A play in which the offensive player makes a *jab step* in one direction and then follows it by driving by the defender in that direction.

Jab step: A short (6 to 8 inches) out-and-back step by an offensive player to see how the defender reacts.

Jump ball: A procedure used to begin a game. The referee tosses up the ball in the center circle between two opposing players, who jump up and try to tip it to a teammate. Also called the "opening tip."

Jump hook: A variation of the traditional *hook shot* in which the shooter takes the shot with both feet in the air.

Jump shot: A shot in which the shooter faces the basket and releases the ball after jumping into the air.

Jump stop: The action of coming to a complete stop, legs apart and knees bent, when dribbling or running; can be a one-foot or two-foot jump stop.

Junk defense: See *combination defense*.

Lane: The rectangular painted area between the *end line*, the *lane* lines, and the *free throw line*. Also called the "paint."

Layup: A shot taken next to the basket in which the shooter extends her arm, lifts her same-side knee, and aims the ball at the upper corner of the painted square on the backboard.

Loose-ball foul: A foul committed when neither team has possession of the ball.

Low post: The area on one side of the basket around the *block*.

Man: The player a defender is assigned to guard. Also short for *man-to-man defense*.

Man offense: See *man-to-man offense*.

Man-to-man defense: A team defense in which each defender guards a specific player or *man*. Also called "player-to-player defense."

Man-to-man offense: A team offense used against man-to-man defenses. Also called *man offense*.

Midcourt line: See the *half-court line*.

Mirror the ball: To follow the movement of the ball with your hands when closely guarding a player who is *pivoting*.

Moving pick: A violation that happens when a screener leans or moves after setting a *screen*.

Net: The cord lacing that hangs down from the rim.

Nonshooting foul: A foul committed against a player who is not in the act of shooting.

Nothing but net: An expression that means the shot swished through the basket without touching the rim.

Off-ball screen: A *screen* set on a defender guarding an offensive player who doesn't have the ball. Also called a "player screen."

Offensive rebound: A *rebound* at the basket a team is attacking.

On-ball defense: Defense that occurs when a defender guards the player with the ball.

On-ball screen: A screen set on a defender guarding an offensive player who has the ball.

One-and-one: Free throws awarded to a team once it's opponent has committed seven personal fouls. If the shooter's first free throw is successful, she shoots a second free throw.

One-Guard Offense: A team offense used against zones with two-guard fronts (2-3 and 2-1-2 zones).

Open stance: The stance used to play *help-side* defense (feet apart, body balanced, knees bent, arms out).

Outlet: (1) To pass the ball after a defensive *rebound* to start the *fast break*. (2) The player who stays in the backcourt to receive an *outlet pass*.

Outlet pass: An *overhead pass* thrown by a defender that starts the *fast break*.

Overhead pass: A two-handed pass thrown from above the player's head.

Overtime: A 5-minute extra period played when the game is tied at the end of regulation play.

Paint: See *lane*.

Palming: See *carrying*.

Pass fake: See *ball fake*.

Personal foul: A penalty assessed on a player who commits an illegal action.

Pick: See *screen*.

Pick-and-roll: A two-person play in which one offensive player sets a screen (*pick*) on the ball handler's defender and cuts (*rolls*) to the basket after the ball handler drives by the screen. Also call a "screen and roll." A common play in college and the pros.

Pivot: The action when the player with the ball spins on one foot and steps with her other foot to protect the ball from a defender.

Pivot foot: The foot that the offensive player spins on while pivoting.

Player-control foul: A nonshooting offensive foul.

Player screen: See *off-ball screen*.

Player-to-player defense: See *man-to-man defense*.

Point guard: (1) A position played by a team's primary ball handler, the player who brings the ball up the court and begins the offense. Also called the 1. (2) The player who plays that position.

Post: (1) A player who plays in and around the *lane* area. A *center* or a *forward* (a "4" or a "5"). (2) An area of the court, as in the *low post* or the *high post*.

Post up: (1) An offensive move in which an offensive player (usually a *forward* or a *center*) positions herself close to the basket with her back toward the basket and the defender behind her so the offensive player can receive a pass. (2) To make that move.

Power forward: (1) A position played by the larger of the *forwards* on the floor, usually a good scorer and rebounder. Also called the "4." (2) The player who plays that position.

Power layup: A two-footed *layup*.

Press: (1) See *full-court press*. (2) To engage in a full-court press.

Press break: A team offense used against a press defense. Also called *press offense*.

Press offense: See *press break*.

Primary break: A *fast break* that involves only a few players from each team.

Pump fake: See *shot fake*.

Push pass: A one-handed *air pass*.

Putback shot: A shot taken on the *rebound* of a missed shot.

Quicks: A slang term used to describe how quick a player is, as in "Darnelle has average quicks."

Rebound: (1) A missed shot that comes off the backboard or rim. (2) To fight for and gain control of a missed shot that comes off the backboard or rim.

Rejection: A blocked shot.

Reserves: See *substitutes*.

Retreat step: A step in which the defender's back foot steps toward the basket, and the lead foot slides in place.

Runner: A shot that a player shoots while running, without taking the time to set up the shot. Also called a "floater."

Safety: The offensive player at the top of the circle.

Sag: A tactic in which a defender leaves her *man* or *zone* and drops into the *lane* to help protect the basket.

Screen: A play in which an offensive player runs over and stands in a stationary position next to a teammate's defender to free up the teammate to dribble or to receive a pass.

Screen away: To pass in one direction and set a *screen* for a teammate in the opposite direction.

Screener: A player who sets a *screen*.

Secondary break: A *fast break* that involves most of the players from each team.

Set play: A sequence of player and ball movement that has an end.

Shooting foul: A violation that happens when a defender fouls the shooter.

Shooting guard: (1) A position played by a perimeter player who is usually the team's best outside shooter. Also called the "2." (2) The person playing this position.

Shot clock: The clock used to limit the time allowed to attempt a shot. Shot clocks are used in pro and college games, but not in middle school and youth league games.

Shot clock violation: A violation that occurs when the team with the ball doesn't get a shot off during the allotted time. It results in a change of possession.

Shot fake: A movement in which the player with the ball acts as if she's about to shoot. It is designed to trick the defender into straightening up, allowing the player with the ball to dribble past her. Also called a "pump fake."

Sideline: The line at each side of the court that marks the boundary of the playing surface.

Sideline play: A play used by the offensive team to put the ball back in play from the *sideline*.

Sixth man: The first *substitute* that comes off the bench to replace a starter.

Skip pass: An *overhead pass* from one side of the court to the other over the defense.

Soft hands: A term used to describe a player who has good hand control with the ball, that is, who is a good passer and receiver.

Speed dribble: A dribble maneuver in which the player pushes the ball ahead of her and bounces it at chest height.

Spin dribble: A dribbling maneuver in which the player does a reverse *pivot* while bringing the ball around her so it ends up in her other hand.

Square up: To pivot so the shoulders and feet face the basket. Also called "face up."

Steal: (1) To intercept a pass and gain possession of the ball. (2) The name for the action.

Stop-and-go dribble: See *hesitation dribble*.

Stop and pop: An offensive move in which a player comes to a sudden stop, picks up her dribble, and shoots the ball.

Strong side: See *ball side*. The opposite of "weak side."

Substitute: A player who comes in the game to replace another player. Also called a "sub."

Swing step: A step in which a defender makes a reverse *pivot* by swinging her lead foot behind the back foot.

Switch: A movement in which two defenders change the offensive player each is guarding.

Technical foul: A violation, such as a player or coach using profanity, that results in the other team getting free throws and possession of the ball. Also called a "T," as in "T him up."

10-second call: A violation that occurs when a team is unable to advance the ball over the midcourt line before 10 seconds have elapsed.

3-point arc: A line drawn on the court 19 feet, 19 inches from the basket. Field goals scored from outside the arc count 3 points. Also called "3-point line."

3-point line: See *3-point arc*.

3-point shot: A shot taken from outside the *3-point line*.

3 points the old-fashioned way: Scoring 3 points by making a 2-point shot, being fouled in the process, and making the *free throw*.

3-second call: A violation that occurs when an offensive player remains in the lane for 3 or more seconds.

Trailer: An offensive player, usually a *center* or a *power forward*, who trails the first wave of players on the *fast break*.

Transition: A movement that occurs when a team changes from offense to defense ("defensive transition") or from defense to offense ("offensive transition").

Trap: A defensive move in which two defenders guard the player with the ball by forming a V with their bodies.

Traveling: A violation that occurs when the player with the ball takes too many steps without dribbling. This is a common occurrence with young players.

Triangle-and-two: A combination defense in which three defenders play *zone* in a triangle formation and two defenders guard specific players *man-to-man*.

Triple threat position: The bent-knees stance that allows the player three options: dribble, pass, or shoot.

Turnover: A loss of possession of the ball caused by a *steal*, an offensive foul, a *held ball*, a poor pass.

Two-Guard Offense: A team offense used against zones with one-guard fronts (1-2-2 and 1-3-1).

Two-shot foul: A violation that occurs when a defender fouls the shooter, and the shot misses. The shooter is awarded two *free throws*.

Up screen: An offensive play in which a player comes from the *low post* area to set a *screen* for a player in the *high post* area.

V-cut: An offensive play in which a player on the perimeter steps toward the basket, drawing the defender with her, and suddenly *cuts* to the perimeter for a pass. The opposite of a *backdoor cut*.

Weak side: See *help side*.

Wing: (1) The area on the court where the *3-point arc* meets the *free throw line extended*. (2) The offensive player who plays in that area.

Zone defense: A team defense in which players are assigned to guard specific areas of the court.

Zone offense: A team offense used against a *zone defense*.

Index

Numbers in **bold** refer to pages with illustrations. The glossary has not been indexed.

Acknowledgments

I'd like to thank the women's basketball staff at North Carolina: Andrew Calder, Assistant Head Coach; Tracey Williams-Johnson, Assistant Coach; Charlotte Smith-Taylor, Assistant Coach; and Greg Law, Director of Operations. Without them, our teams wouldn't have had the success they have had.

I'd also like to thank Jerry Green, former Head Men's Coach at Tennessee and Oregon, former Assistant Men's Coach at UNC-Asheville, and former Varsity Boys' Coach at Hunter Huss High School in Gastonia, NC. Jerry's advice, support, and friendship have been invaluable to me over the years.

Lastly, I'd like to thank all my former players at the University of North Carolina and Francis Marion University. I've been blessed to have had the privilege of coaching such outstanding young women.

About the Authors

Sylvia Hatchell has been a college head coach for 30 years and has accumulated a career win-loss record of 684–266. For the last 19 years, she has coached the University of North Carolina's women's teams to a record of 412–186. Her teams have won five Atlantic Coast Conference titles, and in 1994 her team won the NCAA National Championship. Prior to coaching at North Carolina, she coached at Francis Marion University, where she had a record of 272–80. She led her teams to the AIAW (Association of Intercollegiate Athletics for Women) National Championship in 1982 and the NAIA (National Association of Intercollegiate Athletics) National Championship in 1986. She was inducted into the Women's Basketball Hall of Fame in 2004.

Coach Hatchell lives in Chapel Hill with her son, Van, and her husband, Sammy, who coaches their son's team. She can think of no other place she'd rather live in than Tar Heel Country.

Jeff Thomas, a long-time writer and former Contributing Editor to *Sailing* magazine, has published dozens of articles on sailing and sports. He has coached youth league, AAU, and high school girls' basketball for 18 years and is currently the Varsity Head Coach at Saint Gertrude High School in Richmond, Virginia. In his mind, his teams have won many national championships.